If You Don't Know This, You Don't Know Jack

What A Woman Should Know About A Man

Tonya Nicol Davis

For more information:
Lady Intelligence, Ltd.
www.ladyintelligence.com

ISBN-13: 978-0990371816
ISBN-10: 0990371816

Published 2014
CreateSpace - An Amazon Company

This book is available at special quantity discounts for bulk purchases for sales promotions, premiums, fund-raising, or educational use. Special books, or book excerpts, can also be created to fit specific needs.

For details write:
Lady Intelligence, Ltd.
PO Box 24815
Lyndhurst, OH 44124
Attn: Special Markets
Or visit: www.ladyintelligence.com

To All Daughters

~

~ Keep on Living ~

TABLE OF CONTENTS

INTRODUCTION

While we were preparing my father's obituary, I was in awe that my parents were together for almost 60 years. I was married twice and both marriages lasted less than seven years all together.

In 2012, I wrote the book, "Big Girl Little Girl - Everything I Can Think Of Right Now To Tell You About Life, Money, Credit, Boys, Men, and Sex," which is now a retired title and no longer in print. I wrote that particular book out of reflection, frustration, disgust, and irritation of how life can be mismanaged either out of naivety or by just plain ignorance. I wrote the book with my daughters in mind because I wanted them to have a much greater awareness of how one choice or action over another choice or action could significantly affect the rest of their lives.

I realized two things about those marriages. First, I called myself doing the right thing given the circumstances. But in actuality, I did the wrong thing – I got married. I got married strictly for noble reasons. Second, I knew very, very little about my children's fathers.

In spending tens of thousands of hours in school and in church, I cannot recall a curriculum or doctrine that taught *specifically* on cultivating healthy relationships, the purpose of dating, how to conduct oneself during dating, how to avoid the pitfalls of dating, and what to learn about a man when dating.

In preparing the final chapter of "Big Girl Little Girl," I listed every area that I could think of at that moment where a woman could or should know about a man. At that time, at least 184 areas were determined.

In 2013, Lady Intelligence, Ltd. launched the "Getting to Know Him Better Awareness" campaign geared for females of all ages who entertain a romantic and/or physical relationship with a male. The "If You Don't Know This, Then You Don't Know Jack" chapter addressed what many females do not know or do not think about trying to know while cultivating a relationship with a male – at least the areas that women should definitely know or have some sort of a solid idea about before allowing a man to take up space in her mind, heart, home, and especially in her body.

The mission of the "Get To Know Him Better" campaign is not only to stomp out unplanned pregnancies, but also to minimize the number of single-parent households, to reduce the poverty rate by encouraging abstinence until financially, mentally, and emotionally able to bring a child into the world, as well as to eliminate the spread of sexually transmitted diseases, domestic abuse, and violence amongst women and their children, families, and friends by someone they were just merely dating or their significant other.

We know that relationships are a crapshoot. Knowing everything you can about a man will not make him a prince no more than not knowing anything about a man will make him a monster. The key, however, is to at least make effort to know something about every aspect as much as possible in the early stages of dating.

I know many professional women, including myself, who had homes, stability, A-1 credit, and financial footing when they were alone but then lost it all while they were in a relationship. Some of these losses can be attributed to economic change. But, the majority of the losses are attributed to co-mingling money and having living arrangements with someone who did not share the same practices and philosophies when it came to money and living arrangements. Those practices and philosophies were not learned until after the fact – which is too late.

There are countless news reports of professional women who have been killed or severely beaten by their husbands or boyfriends. In some of those cases, their children, friends, and family members were also injured, abused, or murder victims.

This is not to say that professional women are a higher or more privileged class of women. This is to say that no matter what so-called socioeconomic class a woman falls into, it all comes down to that all women must take the time to know who they allow into their minds, souls, hearts, and bodies. Just because he wears a suit, does not mean he is or he will be Man of the Year.

There is not a prescribed timetable attached to the content in this book and of course, it should be obvious to know certain things before a relationship reaches a certain level of commitment or intimacy. However, the importance is not on when to know, but on knowing as much as there is to know at every opportunity on a consistent basis. The purpose of this book is not to try to find the worst-case scenario or to preach that men are always out trying to play a woman. This book is just an invitation to women to take more time to know a man. This book is not a how-to guide on how to find out everything about a man to turn around and use what was learned to try to get him or manipulate him into a relationship.

Anytime a woman meets a man, it is her responsibility to keep her future in mind. They say that there is nothing wrong with hanging out and having fun. But there is still a component of choice that must prevail the notion to just hang out and have fun.

A woman's actions will always indicate her choice whether she believes she consciously made a choice or not. Women pick the men who have a good chance of being their children's fathers when they decide to enter into an intimate relationship with them. Women pick the men who can have access to their personal information when they divulge everything to him about their lives. Women pick the men who will be around their children and relatives when they invite the men over.

Wise people open the door into their home for guests that they know pretty well – at least as best as they can know.

Whether the goal was for a good time or for something serious, the woman is always the hostess and the gatekeeper at her front door.

Is it possible to know everything about every man that you meet? No. But it is possible, logical, and sensible to explore what you can learn about him in each area discussed in this book. And if you don't? You really won't know him at all.

THE TRUE ANSWERS BEGIN WITH YOU

Have you ever seen or heard of a woman destroying a man's possessions like throwing bricks through his home or car windows, slashing his tires, stalking him or another woman, or destroying another woman's property?

Have you ever seen a single young mother alone with three or more children all under the age of six standing in the rain or frigid cold waiting for the bus?

Is there a woman that you know who has been divorced multiple times?

What about a woman who cries and complain about the men in her life who "don't ever do right"?

These four women are examples of women who did not know what they thought they knew about "their" man. More importantly, they more than likely had not taken the time to know themselves and consider their own destinies.

Anytime a woman loses it over a man, has a bunch of children by a man or more than one man with no commitment, gets married and divorced like it is dating, or becomes obsessed about what a man is doing or not doing, it is because she made the man and/or the relationship the central focus of her existence. The man and/or the relationship was her sun and moon that rose and fell from day in to day out.

**A woman MUST first make the sun and moon
rise and fall upon HER.**

It is highly likely that the women described previously:
- gave all what they thought they should to keep the relationship
- believed the man cared about them as much as they cared about him
- based their own present and future upon his presence in her life
- believed that his presence and future was based upon their being in his life
- believed in what he told them (while blinded to what he <u>really</u> <u>showed</u> them)

When a woman deems her worth outside of herself, this is where she will always be volatile, imbalanced, and left holding the bag of debt and raising children alone.

This is not to say that every woman who is in debt and/or is a single mother did not have any self worth. There are other unforeseen situations out of one's control that can create debt and single parenthood. However, a woman who has no self-worth would most likely wind up in debt and raising children (possibly by different fathers) alone.

There is no way a woman could ever be in a healthy relationship with a man until she is healthy within herself.

If a woman:
- Has a feeling of emptiness
- Always feels that something is missing
- Has no specific goals
- Has no standards
- Has no specific boundaries
- Has little to no self-esteem
- Has little to no respect and regard for her health, welfare, and future
- Has little to no regard for the true welfare and care of her children or future children
- Has no game plan or road map...

...she will always go wherever the wind blows due to lack of self-direction and self-control.

TWO IMPORTANT AREAS IN A WOMAN'S LIFE

The two most important areas in a woman's life do not include having a relationship status. The sun and moon in a woman's life are:

Her Health and Her Finances

Health and money are the two things that women must have with or without a man to take care of not only herself but as well as her children, if applicable.

A Woman's Health

Every woman MUST have an established relationship with the following health practitioners:

Primary Care Physician ~ to receive an annual physical exam, blood pressure check, and biochemistry blood work to make sure all levels are within normal range i.e. glucose, HbA1c, lipid assessment, ALT, thyroid profile, etc.

Obstetrician/Gynecologist ~ to receive yearly pelvic, breast, and reproductive organ examinations; prenatal care during pregnancy; sexually transmitted disease prevention and tests; and birth control consultation and prescription. Obstetricians, Gynecologists, and OB/GYN nurse practitioners are very instrumental in discovering conditions in other areas of the body and making referrals to other specialists for life-saving treatment measures.

Dentist ~ for teeth cleaning every six months; tooth decay prevention or treatment; gum disease prevention or treatment; and dentures, if needed. The dentist will give recommendations to other dental specialties such as to an orthodontist to straighten teeth or to an oral surgeon to remove impacted wisdoms. A beautiful smile and sweet smelling breath captures a man's attention.

Specialists ~ for ongoing quarterly or six month visits as required or dictated by the specialist if under medical care for a specific medical condition. Examples of these specialists would be: endocrinologist, neurologist, pulmonologist, oncologist, etc.

Areas of Health Often Overlooked

A woman's health is more than just about her body. A woman needs to ensure that not only her physical health is together, but also that three other areas that make up her health as a whole are well.

Mental Health ~ to ensure rational thinking and actions; mature perception and reality perception; as well as treatment or prevention for issues such as depression, paranoia, schizophrenia, bipolar, etc. If need be, a woman must establish a close and trusted relationship with someone certified/licensed in the area of mental health who can not only provide treatment services, but can provide a referral to available programs and services as a supplement to a regular visit schedule.

Emotional Health ~ a service provider that specializes in mental health can also give support to a woman's emotional health. Healing that has not taken place regarding feelings or emotions about past incidents can cause mental health issues. A specialist who is gifted in providing support in emotional and mental health is a blessing.

Spiritual Health ~ is more than going to a place of worship. A woman's spiritual health is regulated through an awareness of peace, fulfillment, joy, abundance, prosperity, and faith within herself and her soul. A prayer partner, a holistic health service provider, and a regular daily practice of study, prayer, and meditation all help to firm and solidify a spiritual core.

Sources for spiritual growth is a personal aspect of health where a woman must discern carefully before following any doctrines, creeds, or practices - even if learned during childhood.

Spirituality is an individual practice. Spirituality is not a passed down from momma practice. When a woman finds peace within herself, that is the determining factor that she is living a healthy spiritual way of life. A woman with strong spiritual health is more likely to keep focus on what is real and what is important when it comes to who and what she introduces into her life and into the life of her children, family, and friends.

Lastly, a strong spiritual base is the driving component to a healthy mental and emotional state. When the mental, spiritual, and emotional states are on track, a woman takes better care of her physical state.

A Woman's Money

Financial health is a vital component in a woman's life. If a woman is concerned about feeding her children, then that is a worry that may cause a lapse in judgment.

If a woman has a health condition that will require her to take off of work with no sick time or short term disability, then that is a worry that may cause a woman not to see the other aspects of her life clearly.

If a woman's car breaks down and she is already unemployed with no other transportation to look for a job, then that is a worry that can cause a woman to fall into a state of desperation.

There are only a few choices a woman has to have income. The choices are either:

- Working for somebody – As an Employee for an Employer

- Working for herself – Self-employment

- Having or owning a business with others working with her as staff or team members for the business – Business Owner

- Being an investor in either real estate, businesses, or investment funds - Investor

Working for Somebody - An employee is the term for those who work for somebody else – the employer. The employer pays the employee what the employer deems should be paid based on company needs. Usually, the salary is based upon the position in the organization. The employer always dictates the final salary no matter how hard an employee works and no matter how loyal and dependable the employee has been.

Usually, the people in the organization who gets paid the most are the people who spent a lot of money to go to school to get a degree or certificate saying that they were qualified for that particular position.

The people who get paid the least are the people who do not have the piece of paper saying that they are qualified and they are generally the ones who do the grunt work that supports the company.

The lesser paid are the people doing the work that keeps the company afloat by following the instructions from the people who get paid well to tell the people doing all the work what to do.

For example, the nursing assistant does the hard, hands-on, physical work of taking care of the patient. The nurse gives the patient the meds and tells the nursing assistant what to do next for the patient.

The administrative assistant keeps the executive on task with the executive's schedule, meetings, and project deadlines. The administrative assistant makes sure the executive is handling his/her executive business or at least appears to be. The admin <u>may</u> make $50,000, while the executive is making $500,000.

If an employee stops working, does not show up, or gets sick and cannot come in, then that individual will not get paid. An employee is only paid for the time that he or she shows up and does what they are supposed to do per the employer's instructions or for whatever sick leave/disability benefits he or she may be eligible to receive.

Self-Employment - Self-employment is hanging a shingle up and giving out business cards as a real estate agent, a dentist, a beautician, etc. Every sale or service conducted is a one-time deal. Once the house closes, the dentures are done, or the hairstyle is fixed, a self-employed individual gets paid the next time that someone needs the product or service. People do not usually get new houses or dental work done everyday, every week, or every year. They may get their hair done every week or every two weeks and that is for only as long as they can afford it or if they do not find someone else they like better to do their hair.

Self-employment is based on getting paid one time when the work is done and when there is work to do. If there is no product sold or no service rendered – then there is no pay. The money does not come until somebody agrees to invest in the offered products or services - even while the self-employed individual is marketing for more business. If a self-employed person gets sick and cannot work, then the self-employed person is not getting paid. A self-employed person has to keep on going non-stop to keep the money coming in to survive. A self-employed person cannot afford sick days or any time off.

Business Ownership - Business ownership is when there is a team or staff supporting the business owner in the business. The business owner's income is based off the efforts of others.

An attorney or partners will have a law firm or law practice with a team of lawyers. The real estate agent will instead be a broker or own a real estate brokerage with agents helping people buy and sell homes under the broker's name. The dentist will have a team of dental hygienists and dentists to treat clients. The concept of network marketing or multi-level marketing falls under this manner of producing income. An independent contractor that subcontracts work on a regular basis is another example.

A business can either be built from the ground up or may be purchased as an existing business or franchise. An ideal business operates and produces without needing the owner to be present in day-to-day matters.

Investors - Investors direct their money to make more money – i.e. in real estate, to start up businesses, to build existing businesses, stocks, funds, etc.

Net Worth

Every individual who has money coming in and money going out should know their financial net worth.

The formula to determine net worth is:

Assets - Liability = Net Worth

An asset is the value of having something free and clear – equity in a home, cash in the bank, investment portfolios, and so on.

A liability is what is the amount that is owed – auto loans, home loans, credit card debt, etc.

Credit Score

Unless a person is paying by cash, that person is using credit. Good credit means receiving application approvals with favorable rates, prices, and terms. Poor credit means extraordinary high and ridiculous rates, prices and terms or declined applications. The goal is to be 720 or above.

If a woman has excellent credit, she should want the man with whom she may co-mingle money to have excellent credit as well.

For the Children

A woman's financial health must be in top order if she has children. The first thing a woman must do as soon as she learns she is pregnant is to adjust her focus to the protection of her offspring and the preservation of their stability.

A woman must have her financial affairs in order especially when it comes to guardianship and having a financial trustee over the children's welfare and money. The guardian and the financial trustee do not necessarily need to be the same people. The guardian is the person deemed to be best in the day-to-day care of the child or children. The financial trustee is the person who is believed to be the best when it comes to taking care of the child or children's financial needs and care.

Insurance

A life insurance policy is key to financial stability should anything happen. A term life insurance policy should be in place not only to cover you, but your children should be covered under an insurance rider of the family policy as well. The purpose for you to be covered is to continue the income that would be lost so that your children can continue living in the lifestyle in which they were accustomed while not becoming a financial burden for whomever assumes the responsibility of raising them.

The time to get a term life insurance policy is now. Age and health conditions cause increased rates and even worse, insurance application denials.

Last Will and Testament, Health Care Power-of-Attorney, Living Will, and Financial Documents

Every adult, whether or not he or she has children, should have a Last Will and Testament, a Health Care POA, and a Living Will. These are the legal documents that you establish to dictate the course of action you want regarding specific circumstances in time of death or sickness. These specific circumstances include the children's welfare and financial care, property distribution, and your own health care action plan. An attorney who is well informed regarding your state and county laws must prepare these types of documents.

If you have property, be sure to have the survivorship deeds on file with the county. Ensure that all bank accounts and financial funds have beneficiaries listed and that those beneficiaries outlined in the wills correspond to the names on the bank accounts.

A woman must also have in place and easy to find all information regarding any and all retirement and pension plans.

The last thing a woman needs is not to have the care of her children in place should something happen to her. This is of the utmost importance before adding a companion into your home and into the lives of your children.

Legal Health

The blanket of legal protection over all areas in a woman's life is having an attorney that can be accessed at any time.

Almost everything you do is a legal situation.

- When you buy something and do not receive a receipt, that is a legal situation.

- When you purchase a home and/or a car, those are legal situations.

- When you drive a car, when someone drives your car, if you drive someone else's car, those are all legal situations.

- If you get your hair done and then your hair comes out, that is a legal situation.

- When you hire somebody to do work on your car or work in your home, those are legal situations.

- When you buy food from the store and you find out that it is contaminated, that is a legal situation.

- What you post online on social media or send in an email, those are legal situations.

- If you get hurt on someone else's property, that is a legal situation.

- If somebody gets hurt in your home, that is a legal situation.

- When someone enters your home with or without invitation, that is a legal situation.

- Anything and everything that you do for a living is a legal situation.

Every person needs access to legal representation.

Some employers offer access to legal counsel under an elective group coverage to their employees. It may be a good idea NOT to obtain this type of coverage through your employer. If you needed legal counsel regarding your employer, the legal representation obtained through your company could not help you.

It does not make sense for the law firm that the employer contracted to help its employees with legal problems to turn around and help the employee create a formal, legal complaint against the very company that hired them. That would be a conflict of interest. The legal assistance offered through the employer may have a referral mechanism in place for this type of situation. But, it is still better to consult with a firm independent from the employer.

There are legal insurance companies and legal coverage memberships available. Be sure to select coverage or membership that will cover the most important aspects in life such as consumer law, contract review, court representation, traffic law, family law, real estate law, tax law, etc.

Generally, with a legal plan membership, you can call up an attorney and ask questions and not be charged consultation fees. A good legal plan membership company would offer unlimited access to an attorney.

Also, as part of a good legal plan membership, you can be referred to an attorney who specializes in whatever particular area of law that you need. The attorney fees will be discounted - at least they should be discounted - from the normal hourly rate that the firm would have charged to people who are not in the membership.

Remember, every action is a legal situation.

STAY ON COURSE AND NOT ON A WILD GOOSE CHASE

A woman who has it together does not go on many wild goose chases. The saying 'going on a wild goose chase' means in this context 'running around looking for something that will most probably not be found.' Women who go on a wild goose chase are looking for something that they feel is missing in their life, which may include:

- Love

- Religion

- Material Things

- Relief from Pain

- Fulfillment

- Belonging

- Acceptance

- Recognition

- An Escape from Hardship

- An Escape from Grief

- An Escape from Reality

The areas listed previously generally fall in one or more of the three health categories of: Mental, Emotional, and Physical.

Before you can set aside any blinders and get to know a man, **<u>you must first know about you</u>**. You must continually be tuned into you, whether you are single or with someone.

Whether you are or not in a relationship, you must be content and satisfied with whom, where, what, and how you are and with what you have.

If you are still working on you, then you will be trying to work on him - trying to get him "right" or "together" while dragging him off, or at least trying to drag him off, on a wild goose chase with you.

If a woman does not know "herself,"
she will fall for any "him".

DEALBREAKERS

Every person must have a level of standards. Even children can be taught how to create and maintain certain standards in their lives. A standard is the criteria in every aspect of life that must be evident before moving forward. If that standard is not evident, no matter the consequences or reasoning, then that is a dealbreaker.

For example, a dealbreaker could be a certain salary range. If the ideal salary is $40,000 a year, but the prospective employer is offering $35,000 a year maximum, then the decision would be to either accept the job at $35,000 or stick to the ideal salary of $40,000 and keep looking for another job. A salary less than $40,000 is the dealbreaker. A salary of $40,000 is a personal standard.

As it comes to dating, the dealbreaker could be smoking. The man could have everything going for him and wants to give all he has. But, if he lights up a cigarette, cigar, or a joint, it is adios because the woman just cannot stand smoke. She might not smoke herself or she may not like the smell in her house or in her hair. She may not want her children to breathe in any smoke and her children may have respiratory issues where any type of smoke would worsen their condition. Since she does not smoke herself, she may not want to be bothered with ashtrays all around. She could compromise if he is a gentleman and steps outside to light up, but then she may not like kissing someone with the smell of a cigarette or cigar on his breath.

Something a woman just cannot get past is a dealbreaker.

In addition, dealbreakers could be circumstances. If the man is still married, even if he has been separated from his wife for several years, that could be a dealbreaker. In fact, it should be a dealbreaker. Another dealbreaker could be if his family members are meddlesome in his personal and private affairs.

A dealbreaker is whatever a woman would not live with even if the man walked on water.

Other examples that could and probably should be considered a dealbreaker include:

- Addiction to gambling

- Addiction to substance abuse

- Alcoholism

- Addiction to work

- Attachment to momma's apron strings

- Possessing poor credit

- Practicing unhealthy eating habits

- Dependency on others

- Lack of enforcement or demand of respect from family or children

**The dealbreaker is when
you would rather be alone than entertain a relationship with
someone regarding a particular issue.**

DEALMAKERS

Dealmakers are what a woman welcomes in her life when it comes to cultivating relationships.

To be clear on the dealmakers, make a mental note on what experiences you would love to see happen in a relationship with someone. Be sure to make those ideal experiences based on character-based ideals and not on material-based wants. These are very basic examples:

Material or Superficially Based	Character Based
He drives an expensive car.	He insists on opening the door when I get in or out of his car.
He buys me clothes and jewelry.	He shows me that I am important to him by the way he speaks to me.
He pays for my hair to get done.	He likes my style and does not insist on me changing my style or my hair.

Would it be nice if a man bought you clothes and jewelry and paid your spa and salon bills on a regular basis? Of course it would. Women receive that type of treatment with no strings attached all day long. However, that would just be the icing on the cake.

But the icing needs to be on a great tasting cake. The great tasting cake would be made up of respect, kindness, dependability, loyalty, and integrity.

Additional Dealmaker Examples

- He is genuine in relating to my family and children.

- He supports my personal choices and preferences.

- He is respectful of my religious and spiritual beliefs.

- He believes in the same parenting style and practices as I do.

- He does not wish to monopolize my time, but yet he still wants to spend quality time with me.

- If there were an emergency, he would be by my side. He has shown that he is dependable.

THE SOURCE OF DOMESTIC ABUSE

A woman who suffers from any type of abuse most likely came to be believe at some point in her life that she is not worthy to be treated with respect, love, compassion, and consideration. It is safe to say that a woman who can be classified as an abuse victim would most probably be someone with low self-esteem.

Low self-esteem can be hereditary, but many times can be developed by being put down, yelled at, or ridiculed in the earlier stages of life. An adult who accepts abuse was most likely told they were ugly, stupid, non-talented, fat, smelly, not wanted, a pain in the behind, or told some other type of insult. As those insults continued, he or she came to believe those insults and concluded, either consciously or subconsciously, that they were among the chosen not to deserve good things or good treatment. If that person received ridicule from home, school, and work, then that person would most probably have very low self-esteem to the point that may require some type of therapy. This is where having sound emotional, spiritual, and mental health is crucial.

If a woman is not happy with any aspect of her life including her looks, her weight, her hair, her skin color, her shape, her height, her clothes, her finances, her circumstances, then she is not fit to enter into a relationship with someone. Sure, she may find a nice man who could care enough to work through those issues with her. However, if she does not like herself or love herself as she is inside and out, she cannot like or love someone else in a healthy way. It is highly likely that if a woman does not like herself or love herself as she is, she will look at relationships as a fix to her life.

**A woman with low self-esteem with
few to no standards or dealbreakers in place
is a prime candidate
to be in an abusive relationship.**

COURTSHIP

Society's courtship practice has evolved to knowing how good someone is in the bed first before knowing the person's middle or last name. The value of the body has been distorted. The female, especially the young female, is courted daily by marketing to have beautiful hair and skin with a banging body. The media continuously grooms today's young woman that she must be hot, sexy, and free.

As depicted in movies and on TV circa 1920 to 1972, the phases for a long-term relationship between a woman and a man followed this safe, old-fashioned, seemingly now ancient world model:

- Courtship

- Engagement

- Marriage

- Intimacy

- Family

- Death Do They Part

In today's society, the courtship model is:

- Intimacy
- Family
- Maybe a Continued Relationship
- Maybe Marriage
- Possible Divorce

Courtship was designed to provide the time to "get to know him better" following the old-fashioned, seemingly now ancient model.

Entering into courtship is just like driving a car. Courtship is the time to:

- Ride on cruise control to arrive at a wonderful destination,
- Slam on the brakes if driving and get out of the car before it catches on fire, or
- Stop being the passenger with a reckless driver heading toward a horrific crash.

However, the accelerator pedal is NEVER pushed because there is never a reason to push or rush into a relationship.

CONVERSATIONS

Approach conversations with a man on a "need to know" basis. A woman giving all the details about her personal life immediately does three things:

- One - kills all the mystery about her - letting him know all about her without him putting forth an effort to learn about her

- Two - puts a woman at a disadvantage because unless he is a motor mouth, she will not find out as much about him as he knows about her

- Three - if the man was not serious in the first place, then she just made it easy for him to identify what buttons to push to make her jump high because he knows exactly just what she wants to hear and will use that to his advantage.

Your goal in early conversations is to find out as much as you can regarding:

- His Personal Information

- His Childhood

- His Family

- His Finances

- His Profession

- His Health

- His Character

- His Recreational Habits

- His Spirituality/Religion Beliefs or Practices

- His Educational Background

- His Goals/Dreams/Aspirations

You owe it to yourself to know whom you have around you, your children, your family, your friends, your co-workers, and most importantly in your home - let alone in your bed, on your mind, a part of your heart, and accessible to your body.

You most definitely also owe it to yourself to know as much as you can about who you are electing to be the father of your future children.

GAUGING COMPATIBILITY BASED ON MATERIAL THINGS

There is nothing materialistic that can help you gauge a man's compatibility. The only thing that material assets can help identify is possibly his money management skills.

However, if he drives a high-end luxury vehicle and his home is in need of great repair or updates, that is a sign that his financial focus is on outward appearances and not long-term asset building.

Another example is he may dress sharp as a tack but he lives mortgage or rent-free in a family owned residence. He may have great shopping skills, but he does not know how to acquire and maintain a home for himself on his own, let alone for a family.

A woman must be careful not to let material possessions fool her. A man who makes $160,000 a year can lose his job causing his income to drop to nothing. Just the same, a man making $42,000 a year can land an opportunity to make $300,000 a year.

The vehicle that a man drives, the kind of job that a man has, the amount of income that you believe he makes, and the way a man dresses do not mean anything in the real scheme of things. A woman who wants to gauge compatibility, especially financial compatibility, needs to learn about how he manages the unseen – behind closed doors. A man's outside appearance can impress all day long, but it does not tell you the real story. That real story comes from taking the time to learn more about his behaviors, habits, and character.

QUESTIONS TO ASK YOURSELF

A woman has to be firm on her own standards before trying to connect with someone else. If she is not firm on where she is going and what her ideals are, then she will be floundering around wasting time with incompatible men. One of the key purposes to dating is to learn. Another key purpose is not to waste time trying to make something work.

If you are involved with someone incompatible, that incompatibility will block energy and space and will also block an open door for a compatible individual to enter.

It is advantageous if you have clear answers to the questions you will find in this chapter. You must be true and honest with yourself.

The time to know these answers is before trying to learn or getting to know someone else.

These questions are the foundation of what you need to know about yourself before you can ever begin to learn about someone else to determine compatibility. It is one thing to think you know the answers to these questions, but it is an important thing to sit down and study carefully each question with in-depth thought and consideration to arrive to an honest answer.

The only wrong answer is an answer that is not a sincere answer on how you truly feel or believe about a certain area.

Home and Family

Many women find themselves in unhappy situations when they decide to bring everyone including her kids and his kids into one big wanna-be-happy home. Healthy and loving blended families exist today and the world is full of couples sharing their testimonials. However, unhealthy and horrific blended families are just as evident. A torturous living environment is when a woman is deeply involved with an incompatible man because she did not soul search on certain areas.

Ask yourself the following questions:

- Do I want any children or any more children?

- What must be in place before I have any children or any more children?

- Is having children or having more children a priority for me?

- Am I truly ready to be a stepparent?

- Am I interested in having in-laws?

- How involved in a man's life do I believe his family should be or should not be?

- How important is it to me that the potential in-laws and I relate?

- How important is it to me if the potential in-laws have made it clear they are not fond of me?

- Could I ever be happy with a man whose family shows that they do not want him to be involved with me?

- If the in-laws wanted to spend a lot of time with me, am I open to that?

- How much am I willing to contribute as far as time and finances toward the welfare and care of a man's children?

- How do I really feel about his grandchildren?

- Am I willing to adopt if the man and I cannot produce children together?

- How comfortable am I that his children are not particularly fond of me? How would I handle it if his children make it clear that they do not want me around?

- What am I willing to do and what would I prefer he does as far as birth control methods are concerned?

- Am I willing to be permanently sterile or do I wish for my partner to do the honors when the choice comes not to have children or any more children?

Money

Co-mingling money and incompatibility is just like water and oil - they do not mix.

Two people need to be on the same page and on one accord when it comes to finances. Money is the number one argument in relationships.

Ask yourself the following questions and be honest with yourself with the answers:

- Am I a saver or am I a spender?

- To whom do I owe money and what is the total amount that I owe for everything and to everybody?

- What is the exact value of all of my assets?

- What is my current Net Worth?

- What is my current Cash Flow?

- What is my current credit score?

- Is my credit score excellent or poor?

- What financial goals do I have in place?

- Is my current spending and credit utilization consistent toward stability and excellence?

- Do I wish to rent or own a home?

- Where would I like to live in the next five years, ten years, and twenty years?

- Am I open to relocating now or in the future?

- Am I willing to uproot my home and leave family members who live here to follow a man who has to move because of his job?

- Do I have my emergency and retirement plans and funds in place?

- Am I continually contributing to these plans/funds?

- What are my future acquisition and business goals?

- Are my action plans complete for those goals?

- Am I really executing my action plans to achieve those goals?

- Do I have term life insurance coverage for myself?

- Are the children covered with a term life insurance policy?

- Do I have a current Last Will and Testament, Health Care POA, and Living Will in place?

- Would I be willing to sign a prenuptial agreement if asked?

- Do I need to have a prenuptial agreement if I choose to get married?

- Would I be comfortable with a man who is an entrepreneur and not an employee with a regularly scheduled job?

Cohabitation

- Am I really ready to share my living space with another person?

- Am I really ready to share my living space with another person's child or children?

- Do I want my children around his children? Do I see any potential behavior problems or dangers? If there are potential problems, how am I going to address these issues?

- If I decide to build a home with my children, a husband, and possibly his children, how would I want the chores to be distributed in the household?

- What am I willing to do as far as financial and physical upkeep of the home with a new husband and/or his children along with my children (if applicable)?

- Do I prefer to have a home that could be in a magazine or do I prefer to have a home that looks like somebody lives in it?

- Do I want to deal with his children's mothers? Are the children's mothers pleasant or hostile?

Relations

A woman cannot move forward in getting to know a man better if she is still holding bitterness and/or still bickering with one of her children's father. A woman cannot wrap her mind around taking the time to get to know another man if she is still hung up on what she still thinks what a man did wrong five years ago.

Ask yourself:

- Do I have any unresolved issues with any ex's and/or with my children's father(s)?

- Do I have a respectful and mature relationship with my children's father(s) as co-parents without bitterness, bickering, bantering, or jealousy?

- Do I have any hang ups or trust issues about men in general?

Sexual Intimacy

- How many times during the week would I wish to be intimate with a committed partner?

- Would I be willing to be in an open relationship?

- Am I open to participate in a man's sexual fantasies, i.e. a threesome?

- If I am struggling with my sexual orientation, am I able to be honest with a man about my sexuality?

- Do I have anything that I should disclose about my sexual history or sexual health prior to a sexual encounter with a new partner?

Spiritual and Political Views

Discussion regarding religion and politics is known to cause conflict and heated debates. Be clear on where you stand when it comes to personal religious/spiritual beliefs AND political viewpoints.

Ask yourself:

- Am I currently fulfilled regarding my religious practices and spiritual beliefs?

- Am I open to learning about another's religious doctrine and incorporating some of their practices?

- Is it important that he shares the same religious practices and spiritual beliefs as I?

- What is important to me about today's political climate?

- Is it important that the man in my life is affiliated with the same political party as I?

- What is my level of participation in political government and elections?

- Should he be as active or inactive in political government as I?

Vibes

No matter how nice a man seems, a woman has an internal indicator, which is called intuition, that will let her know if it is okay to move forward or if she should quickly leave him alone.

You must be in tune with your intuition, listen to your intuition, and then respond accordingly so.

It cannot be stressed enough that a woman must keep the focus on finding out more about the man before she broadcasts every single major and minor detail about her life to him - especially before becoming intimate with him.

Questions to ask yourself and to remember to ask yourself again and again as time goes on include:

- Do I feel safe around him?

  If a man shows the slightest chance of aggression, that is the loudest message that you could ever receive that he is definitely not the man for you. There is no room in a healthy relationship for aggression of any kind.

- Am I confident around him as an equal or do I take the back seat and let the man drive?

  If you take the back seat and allow him to drive, you must determine if: 1) it is because it is a mutual agreement that a woman should be submissive to the man, 2) it is because you do it out of fear of harm or intimidation, or 3) it is because you have low self-esteem. In all actuality, all three are signs that trouble may be ahead. Definitely, the latter two are unacceptable and propose a clear message that you should stop seeing that man immediately and begin to build your self-esteem before ever entertaining another relationship.

- Am I capable of supporting someone's dreams and decisions while maintaining support of my own dreams and standards?

  It can be difficult to bring contribution and support to someone else's dreams when your plate is full of your own projects and other accountabilities. A woman does no one any good when she is overwhelmed and pushes through just to push through to the point of exhaustion, stress related ailments, and/or resentment.

- Am I able to give toward the relationship effortlessly?

  A relationship should be a joy. If a woman is in a relationship and is huffing and puffing to make a man happy, she is in the wrong relationship or she is doing the wrong thing to be in the relationship. Although, they say a healthy relationship is work, it really should not be. When a relationship goes through a rocky season, it would be helpful to figure out if that season is a sign that the relationship is over or if it is a sign that one partner or both partners should naturally do something differently.

- What exactly are the dealmakers and the dealbreakers for you?

  You must know what your dealmakers and dealbreakers are far before you begin to entertain a relationship with a man. If you do not know these things beforehand, then as been stated throughout this book, you will bend to wherever the wind shall blow.

It's Complicated

You must answer, "Yes!" to the following question:

- Am I legally single?

There is no valid reason for a married or separated woman to cultivate a relationship with a man if she is legally tied in marriage to someone else. Legally separated still means married. A legal separation is not a divorce. A legal separation still bounds the two with a resolution yet to be made - reconciliation or dissolution.

A married or separated woman has no legitimate right to expect a man to be fully committed to her because she is not coming to the table legally or morally able to make a true commitment herself.

Many married people get together with someone else and once they decide to move on, they eventually divorce so that they can be with their new love without baggage.

However, why have an unresolved matter lingering? A woman serious about her time minimizes any potential for drama by addressing unresolved matters immediately.

There is no reason to have a relationship where 'it's complicated.' If the relationship is already complicated, then the last thing to do is to add another party to include more complications and confusion.

BEFORE MOVING FORWARD

Spending time outside of the bedroom and in the midst of activities, friends, family, and various social events is the ultimate way of learning more about someone. If a man just wants to spend time with you at your home or in his home in an intimate atmosphere, than that relationship is solely based and most likely will remain solely based on a sexual relationship.

Learning the various aspects as noted in this book will come from observation. No man wants to be interrogated, so conducting a straightforward Q&A is not the way to learn more about a man.

There may be some times when a man tells you things that are just flat out lies. Everybody does not reveal everything about themselves either because they are not comfortable and need to know the person better themselves or basically, they just do not have that intention in doing so.

The purpose of this book is for a woman to get to know a man better - especially the man whom she is entertaining to extend an invitation into her living space, her mind, her time, her heart, her body and into the lives of her family. With that being said, it is okay to search public records while observing his behaviors with families, friends, colleagues, and associates - especially with children.

The second purpose of this book, very well the most important actually, is for a woman to know herself better. The very things she wants to know about a man, she should have a firm answer about her own stand in those areas.

If there is anything to take away from the content in this book, it is:

- The five important qualities that a man must bring to the table: 1) Stability 2) Tranquility (Peace and Joy) 3) Maturity 4) Responsibility, and 5) Dependability. If a man does not bring at least these five principles to the table, then it would be wise to step back, re-evaluate, learn more, then follow your gut. A definite dealbreaker is having any inkling of unease. Try not to sell yourself short and second-guess what you see that appears on your dealbreaker list.

- What you see is what you get.

- Determine if his habits, practices, lifestyle, and/or beliefs either mesh or collide with your own habits, practices, lifestyle and/or beliefs. It must be a mesh, not a conflict.

- There is no changing a man, there is no persuading a man, and there is no so-called "training" a man.

- Take what he says and what he does for what it is.

- A man changes his mind when HE wants to change his mind.

- There is nothing CUTE about a grown man. Murderers, thieves, rapists, and child molesters can appear to be 'cute' or attractive at first. An intelligent, together, grown woman does not think a grown man is 'cute' and does not allow a man's attractiveness cloud her judgment. An intelligent, together, grown woman looks to see if a man is compatible and if his behaviors, habits, and characteristics appear as dealmakers and not dealbreakers – whether he is fine or not.

- Stick to your own principles regarding domestic and financial related matters.

- There is nothing that a woman can do to make a man talk about a topic that he does not want to talk about. If that topic is important to her, but yet he does not budge, this is where she must be honest with herself. If it is a topic or you have questions where you really want to know the answers and it bothers you because he is not freely answering those questions, then you must decide your next choice – continue not to receive a direct and honest answer or leave him alone. The door is always open to leave an unsettling position.

- There is not one thing too private for a man not to share when you are sexually involved with him, when having him around your family and children, and/or when you are contemplating any type of financial relationship with him.

- A woman has to know herself in and out before she can discern any outside nonsense.

- The search you conduct for more information is not to use to cast down judgment, but to measure if his habits and patterns are compatible with your own.

- A woman must never hang everything upon a man's word about everything - especially in the beginning. Again, it is not all on what a man says. It is on what he does.

AREAS TO LEARN ABOUT

His Personal Background

What is his full name (Jr., Sr., II, III)?

As crazy as this may sound and just as ludicrous to mention, everyday women meet men and obtain just his first name (or just the name that he gives her). By the end of the week, the man has been in her home, around her family and children, eaten her food, helped himself to anything in the house from the refrigerator to command control of the TV remote, and is the king in her bedroom.

Then in the next few days, when he ignores her calls and she puts someone up to call to see if he answers, she finds herself devastated - wondering what happened.

The answer to what happened is that she did not have self-respect. She gave her body to a stranger. The least that a woman must do is have a man's full legal name.

If a man hesitates one second to give his full name, then that is the first red flag and really the only flag needed for a woman to keep it moving. There should be no reason why a grown man must think about giving out his whole name. This is a dealbreaker.

Any man who is afraid to give his last name has something to hide. If he is so-called cautious to sharing his full name to someone he has just met, then he has no business stepping up to an attractive, intelligent, lovely, classy, drama-free woman, such as yourself, asking for your name. It does not matter whatever reason he gives in not sharing his last name. There are no second chances for a man to tell a woman his full name.

Now on the other hand, a woman is not feel obligated to give out her full name because she does not know the man from Adam. Anyone's full name is easily searchable on today's Internet. By giving out your name, this is all "Jack" needs to do to know all about you. "Jack" can now pull up where you live, your family members' names, family photos and info about where you work from your social media sites, public court documents, etc.

If the man has a problem with you not sharing with him your last name, then that is the first sign of disrespect because he is not respecting your philosophy about not giving out your last name to just anyone who asks.

Disrespect of any kind is second on the dealbreaker list. However, getting to know someone is supposed to be fun, not an FBI operation with strategic tactics. However, if a man is indeed taken aback with you for not sharing your full or last name, keep it moving and keep it moving quickly. A man having a problem about a woman not disclosing her name to someone she has just met is potentially dangerous.

In today's times, you must be careful when going out. If a man asks you for your phone number or name, it is not necessary to be flippant when you do not wish to be bothered. Politely turn down is advances and do not give him a wrong phone number to make him go away. Unfortunately, women have lost their lives turning down a man's advances.

If a man shares only a nickname or street name, keep it moving from there as well. The name that you want is the name on his birth certificate, driver's license, or state ID.

Is he married, separated, legally separated, or divorced?

Marcy did not find out James was still married until after she wore his engagement ring around his family and children for two months. James finally told Marcy he was tired of her pressing him to pick a date and that he still had to get his divorce. Marcy had been going on James' word that he was divorced from the mother of his children. James has been married for 22 years. Marcy and James had been dating for two years.

Laura met Malcolm at her new job just two weeks after she started. The two began going out to the lake, to restaurants, to the movies, etc. Laura repeatedly asked Malcolm if he was married and Malcolm consistently said that he was divorced. Laura kept asking because she kept looking into the public records for the divorce decree and could not find it. After several months had passed and Laura had fallen madly in love with Malcolm, something told Laura to look up marriage licenses. Laura also decided to look up marriage information because Malcolm seemed to always avoid sharing basic information about his ex-wife like even her name. Laura never probed for more information because Malcolm never wanted to talk much about his personal history and always changed the subject. Laura found that Malcolm was indeed still married. Malcolm's wife was Laura's ex-husband's uncle's wife's daughter. Laura never met them when she was married to her ex-husband.

The second thing for you to find out after his full name is if he is 100% single. Not separated. Not still going through a divorce.

Dating a man that is still in some type of marital situation introduces unnecessary drama into a single woman's life.

Why would an intelligent single woman date a man who is legally tied and bound to another woman? There is nothing that a married man can offer a single woman except temporary satisfaction and string along promises.

For example, Meg and Charles had been seeing each other for a little over a year while Meg has known all along that Charles was married. Meg finds out she is pregnant, but Charles is not leaving his wife. In fact, Charles is not the least bit pleased that Meg is pregnant. Meg's child is born into a single-parent household.

Every single woman deserves to have a 100% single man who is living in his own self-funded home, who has court recorded divorce papers in thoroughly dried ink if he has ever been married, and he is not living with someone other than the children that he is raising.

A single woman has no reason to exchange any conversation other than weather pleasantries until she finds that the man is verifiably single and living alone in his own home.

Only time will give the verifiable truth and the first exchange or greeting is not going to prove he is single unless you search the public records right then and there on your mobile device.

If a man is married, this is what he can offer to a woman who is not his wife:

- Some good sex and that is only if he is good.

- Exposure to an STD (and this can be from any man actually - not just a married man, of course). If a married man is involved with you while cheating on his wife, you are probably not his first or only sidepiece.   Then you will have to question what his other sidepieces and even his wife are doing.

- The heart and body handcuff with broken promises; broken promises to make-up for the broken promises; then money, gifts, and jewelry to lay in the bed with you while he is at home laying in the bed with his wife.

- Possibly a child who will be an emblem of an indiscretion, a potential battleground in co-parenting, and who most likely will grow up wondering why Daddy only spends a minute at the house on Christmas and will get the lesser to nothing than his/her half-siblings receive as far as love and time.

- Suggestion to call roadside assistance and/or the police in case of an emergency, as he will not be available to get away to come.

- Exclusion from ever being a part of his family and social circle. His wife will be his guest as he attends events that have to do with his career, hobbies, place of worship, or any other public events.

- Dinners and movies in other cities and counties to keep from being seen with you.

If he is separated from his wife, this is what he can offer:

- A relationship with you while legally tied to another woman.

If he is single, he can offer:

- A relationship without being legally tied to another.
- Availability if he is serious about pursuing a relationship with you.

How many times has he been married, separated, legally separated and/or divorced?

Donna met Wallace online. They lived in the same city and they began seeing each other exclusively immediately. Wallace has three children by a first marriage and one child by another woman to whom he had never been married. Wallace ensured that he had joint custody of all children and did not pay child support. Although Wallace has joint custody of the children from the first marriage, the children live primarily with their mother. The same with the children of the mother he had never married. Donna and Wallace marry but later divorce after three years. Donna and Wallace have a 2-year-old son. Donna also has a 15-year-old son. Donna files for child support and sole custody and Wallace pays child support as decreed. Wallace rarely comes to see the son he has with Donna. Wallace has since married, divorced, and married again.

Women must pay attention to a man's patterns of how he enters and leaves a relationship as well as how quickly he moves on - even if his own children are involved. In the above story, Wallace has fathered children and moved on leaving three families in a single-parent household situation where six children, including Donna's child by another man, are left without a father figure in the home.

A together single and intelligent woman does not want a man who has a history of leaving one family to begin and live with another. Many children who experience no father in the home are prone to develop low self-esteem and coping issues. A man who has left a family to be with another woman and her family has demonstrated that he could very well leave the new family to begin life with someone else.

How is his financial position as it relates to previous relationships?

If a man has been married before and his marriage lasted at least ten years, the wife of that marriage is entitled to his social security if it is more than what she would get on her own. This is not money out of a woman's pocket if her man's ex-wife receives social security benefits, however.

If a man was married before and the divorce called for his pension to be split with the ex-wife, that could be a problem come time for the man and his new wife to retire. Half of what he could have brought to the table will be going to an ex-wife.

The same with child support arrearages. Any extra money that a man gets is subject to child support if he is in the arrearages. Generally, women who have children and file for divorce, also file for child support - so that support order is already established. If a man receives a tax refund or obtains a lump sum of money such as a retirement payout, that money can get attached to go straight to the child support arrearages. Child support enforcement agencies also attach money from bank accounts. One day, a man has $10,000 in his bank account. The next day he looks up and finds the $10,000 is withdrawn.

What happened was...

If he has ever been married, find out what happened. You must know the truth in what ended his previous marriage(s).

Marla met Tyler at the library. They exchanged numbers and talked on the phone mostly because Tyler wanted to go out after 10:00 PM but Marla was firm that it was time for her to come in the house at that time. During their chats, Marla learned that Tyler had been married three times and all three wives died. Tyler gave legitimate reasons on the causes of their deaths. Marla started to feel sorry for Tyler to have gone through such tremendous loss as he lamented about his misfortune to lose one wife after another. One day, Tyler told Marla that he was picking up a certain chemical for some crazy reason he gave that did not make any sense. Marla knew that the chemical was highly toxic and should be only handled by a professional – a professional that he never said he was. Marla revisited the stories in her head that Tyler told her about his wives' deaths. Marla immediately stopped talking to Tyler. Marla never told Tyler her last name.

Milan told Rachael that all of his former girlfriends and wives hated him. Eventually, Rachael stopped talking to Milan.

Marla and Tyler along with Milan and Rachael are two examples where a women should not only listen to what a man says, but she needs to process what he says.

You need to add up everything a man has said to see if all of the information that he has given to you makes any sense together. If what a man says does not jive, then do not take any precious time to figure it out. He already said what he felt he needed to say or what he slipped up and said. There is no reason to point out any discrepancy he has made or to ask for clarification – especially in the beginning. He already made it crystal clear.

Your initial discernment becomes cloudy when you start asking for clarification and handing out benefits of the doubt.

Once he says something that sounds crazy, it is crazy, and time to go.

A man is a complete stranger until you have spent a considerable amount of time with him in substantial activities – and not in intimate moments. Oftentimes, women who have had intimate moments with a man, especially in the beginning, have the tendency to get fooled into believing that she knows the man very well - because she allowed him to explore her body to 'prove' how into her he is and she has done the same in exchange.

There will never be enough room in your life for confusion.

Marla stuck to her personal rules of dating. She made it up in her mind that dates, especially in the beginning, would be either a lunch or an early evening dinner or movie. Marla knew that she was not ready to be involved in an intimate relationship and refrained from being in certain environments or times of day that would set the mood for that experience. While she was sticking to her personal rules, she used the time on the phone to Tyler to get some history about him. Tyler was nice looking and Marla was not surprised that he had been married multiple times. Marla did not let pity cloud her judgment and attention during conversations because she knows a player tactic is playing on a woman's empathy. She listened to every word Tyler said. When Tyler said he was picking up a poisonous substance, Marla did not need to ask any questions. Tyler had three dead wives and had access to poison. Whether or not Tyler was sincere about what happened to his wives, Marla decided that Tyler was not the man for her without having to go out with him on one date.

Actually, when Marla first found out about the three dead wives, it should have been enough for her, but she slipped and gave benefits of the doubt before she woke up and paid attention to reason.

As far as Milan and Rachael are concerned, Rachael kept in mind that there are two sides to every story. Rachael learned from previous experience that a man who has a collection of angry former girlfriends or wives is a man who has in some way given women an expectation and then flipped the script. Rachael did not want to hang around to be another angry woman in his past.

When Was He Last in Love?

Rebecca met Brian just weeks after Brian stopped seeing Monique. Brian was with Monique for five years. Brian brought up Monique's name in every other sentence about what they used to do together and about little things that Monique used to do.

The key phrase in this question is "last in love". If he was in a recent emotionally involved relationship, determine if his heart is mended and ready for YOUR heart. If a serious relationship is on your agenda, then you need to know if he is ready to move forward wholeheartedly or if he still may have some strong residual feelings about the person before you.

You do not want to date a man who has not had time to move on emotionally, mentally, and physically from another woman.

A man who has not moved on emotionally, mentally, and physically, will be in comparative mode. He will be looking for what you do and do not do to compare to his last love.

Brian showed Rebecca signs from the beginning that he was not over Monique. Rebecca will always be in Monique's shadow at least for several months.

A woman must never knowingly be second in a man's thoughts and heart ever. Leave a man alone who has not moved on from his previous love.

Sexual History Check

When asked about the last time he was in love, a man may answer, "I was with this one woman, but it wasn't serious or meaningful." The relationship might not have been emotionally meaningful to him, but it was most likely sexual. A meaningless relationship does not negate the total count of previous sexual partners.

True Intentions Check

Also, although the relationship might not have been meaningful to him, it may have been meaningful to the woman. An astute woman knows that she herself could have been in the shoes of the woman with whom he classifies as a meaningless relationship.

A man who says that he was in a relationship that was not meaningful or serious is really saying that he spends time with women with no intention or desire to pursue a serious relationship with them or until a woman with whom he is truly interested comes into the picture.

What is his relationship history?

This is a slightly different question in discovering the last time he was in love. This particular question gets into the depth of with whom he has lived, slept with, had children with, accumulated assets with, lost money with, who he left, and who left him. This is more than just the marital ties and legally bound relationships because it encompasses his full history.

You can never know too much about is his last sexual relationship. As noted before, sexual relationships occur with or without emotional involvement. Whether it was meaningful or not, the question yet remains, how many sexual partners has he had in a lifetime? A meaningless relationship does not negate the total count of previous sexual partners.

A woman can learn much from the details of a man's full relationship history if she pays attention and keeps up with the conversation. This type of info provides a woman an opportunity to become familiar with a man's personal patterns when it comes to relationships, parenting, and financial matters.

Going hand in hand with the marital history, if a man has children by different women, again there is the pattern that sets the understanding that he has the ability to create families and then move on to the next. This is not to say that this is what he purposely set out to do because relationships do not work out all the time, as we would want them.

However, history is history. If a person can do it once or more, the easier that he or she can do it again. You are not overly judgmental if you raise your eyebrow at a man who has left households with children when things are not working out - especially if the relationships were no more than two or three years long.

As time goes on, it is easier for a man to walk away from a relationship when walking away has been done once or more before.

Back to Donna and Wallace. He hooked up with Donna after leaving his first wife with the three kids and had the fourth child with another woman that he did not marry. Now, he has the fifth child, a son, with Donna and Donna already had a son. Donna, the first wife, and the woman with the one child are all now single mothers raising Wallace's children alone. Wallace walked away leaving all three women holding the bag to keep a roof over their head and with debt he helped them accumulate. Wallace's exit has affected the lives of three women and six children in just a short period of time.

So many things can come out of just LISTENING and piecing together the relationship history. A man's track record can spin an interesting tale to consider.

What is his true Social Security Number?

The time to know this bit of information is:

- Before having sexual intercourse (pregnancy - may need to file for child support - you never know)

- Before marriage

- Before signing any legal documents including documents for a home (purchase or rental), a vehicle, or any other type of purchase or lease requiring credit and/or signatures

- Before merging health care benefits

Most definitely, a person's social security number is a very private matter and it is illegal to use anyone's social security number for any purpose that has not been authorized in writing by the social security number holder. However, it would be advantageous to have that information recorded prior to the situations just listed previously.

Some men use fictitious social security numbers to avoid garnishment or law enforcement.

When is his birthday?

This is like knowing someone's full name. It is basic information and should not be a mystery unless somebody is trying to hide something. This kind of information should be known at least before a kiss is exchanged or any form of intimacy.

Did he have any pets growing up? What were those pets? What happened to the pet(s)? How were they cared for?

This may seem like a silly little thing to know, but this information begins to establish a little bit about his characteristics, likes, and dislikes.

First, it may give some indication on his capability of caring and caretaking. For instance:

- Did he stick it through in keeping the animals and caring for them until they departed?

- Did he keep his pets until they died or did he have to let them go because he grew up in an unstable household as his family had to move all the time?

- Did he just have them for a short while until he got bored with them?

Second, this is where you can find out if he is allergic to any animals. If a woman loves animals and must have a pet in her home or her children have pets that they dearly love, a woman and the man need to know upfront if he would have difficulty existing in an environment with pets. If having animals is important to you and/or your children, then finding out if the man has an animal allergy is very important.

Raven and Thomas were contemplating building a life together. Raven's son has a dog and Raven's daughter recently obtained a cat. Thomas is allergic to cats. Thomas told Raven that she would have to give up the cat but Raven knows that her daughter would be devastated if she had to give up the cat. Thomas came to resent Raven for not giving up the cat to accommodate his presence in her life.

Does he have any pets now or since being an adult? What were they...what happened to the pets...how were they cared for?

This is primarily the same question but fast-forwarded to the recent past.

What are his feelings about marriage? Is marriage a personal option for him?

A woman needs to find this out early on if it is her desire to be married.

Ericka and Joe met when they were just out of high school. All who knew them expected that Ericka and Joe would marry because they had been dating for almost a decade. However, Joe got married to another woman and had a big wedding. Joe kept coming over to Ericka's home like nothing changed. Ericka was still thinking that one day they would be married until someone told Ericka that they heard about Joe's wedding.

Laura and Malcolm were the couple that met at the job while Malcolm denied he was married and Laura later found out that Malcolm was married to a relative of her ex. Earlier on when they first connected, Malcolm asked Laura if she wanted to get married again. Laura told Malcolm that she did not want to date anybody who was not serious in getting married. Malcolm told Laura that he would consider getting married again. At one point, Laura had all the symptoms of pregnancy and the OTC pregnancy test was inclusive. Laura and Malcolm went to the doctor for a real pregnancy test. Malcolm changes his tune and becomes adamant that he did not want any more children. He informs Laura for the first time that he was already paying child support for five children. While Laura and Malcolm were in the doctor's office, Malcolm was adamant about not wanting to get married.

Learning a man's true desire about marriage is dicey. The word marriage can be used to manipulate the relationship if a man wants to use the woman's desire to get married to his advantage.

The truest feelings and thoughts a man has about marriage come out during a crisis such as a pregnancy scare – much to a woman's disappointment.

It would be ideal if both parties have the capability to have an honest and mature conversation about marriage and children.

What are his feelings about divorce? Does he consider divorce an option?

Marriage was originally designed to be a lifelong commitment. If divorce were an option for a man, than an intelligent woman might ask herself why would marriage to him be an option?

Outcomes of a divorce include:

- Devastated children

- Financial hardship of starting over, moving, rebuilding, etc.

- Poor credit

- Stress

- Emotional and Mental Anguish

Divorce is traumatic to the mind, the heart, the family, and the wallet. Although it is easier to get in a marriage, it is not as easy to get out.

If divorce is an option, so are all the negative outcomes. If divorce is an option, then marriage is never an option.

How does he feel about living together? Is living together a personal option for him?

This falls under general discussion. If you are a woman who is against living with someone while not married to them, this conversation will determine the presence of a dealbreaker or a dealmaker.

Does he want any children?

The best time to know this is fairly early in dating. If a woman is set to have children or have more children, she does not need to spend time with someone who is not interested in having children.

If the man says that he does not want any kids, then there is no changing his mind unless he changes his mine on his own.

It is asinine to try to trap a man by having children. Children do not make a man stay or love.

Has he had a vasectomy?

Hopefully, a man will be upfront with the answer to this question.

Is having children a priority and a must have in his life?

Just as a woman wants children but the man does not, the same as if a woman does not want to have any children or any more children, and the man does.

If you are adamant about not having any children and he expresses a desire to have children, then respect his wishes and let him find the mother of his future children.

How would he feel if you got pregnant?

While in the doctor's office, Laura got the answer from Malcolm in this situation when she thought she was pregnant. Malcolm finally shared his true feelings about beginning a family with her while they were at the doctor's office.

Other questions relating to unplanned pregnancies and/or children:

- What are his feelings about giving a child up for adoption?

- What are his feelings about adopting a child?

- What are his feelings about abortion?

- What are his feelings about aborting his own child?

If you got pregnant today, what would he want to do?

The best time for you to ask this question would be prior to an intimate relationship. He should not have a hesitation in answering. Pay attention to his answer and read between any lines, especially to determine if he is just giving you an answer that he thinks you want to hear.

Other important child related questions:

- What are his feelings about raising kids?

- What are his feelings about disciplining kids? What about disciplining his significant other's kids?

- What are his beliefs about how to build for a child's future?

- If he has kids, what is he doing for their future currently? What would he do or is he willing to do for the future of his significant other's children?

- What do you actually see him doing for his children? How much time does he spend with them?

If he has not been married by now, why not?

A man can be careful about entering into a marriage just as a careful woman and rightly so. On the other hand, if a man is in his 40s or over, he may not ever have been interested in getting married.

An answer that a man may give to this question is, "I haven't found the right one yet."

It may prove pointless to ask, "What would make the right one?" or "How would you know if you found the right one?"

Trust and believe that when a man finds the right one, he will let that woman and the entire world know under no uncertain terms that she is the love of his life.

Some men may use that "I haven't found the right one yet" as part of their player game. A player is a master at offering hope to a woman for something more based on what he has learned thus far about what she wants.

Other things to consider is that some men who have not yet married may be bi-sexual, gay, or trying to figure out just what is their sexual preference.

Lastly, men who are in their 40s and older are oftentimes set in their ways if they have been a bachelor for a long period of time. It may prove to be a difficult adjustment for a long time bachelor to share living space and commit to another individual who has hopes, wants, and needs.

What are the names and ages of his children?

This is an intimate way of knowing a man who is a candidate for a long-term commitment/marriage.

Since the children are a part of him, it is good for a woman not to be shy about knowing more about the children who could possibly be a part of her family. Knowing the names and ages of the children help a woman know a little more about their father in various ways including the timeline of his life on when they were conceived, where he was, where he has been in their life, etc.

Getting to know about the children as a way to get closer to him or to impress him, however, is immature. Even if the man does not say anything, he will smell that a mile away. Secondly, the children, no matter the age, would get a whiff of it too and not take it kindly.

What are the names, ages, and residential areas of his children's mommas?

While Donna and Wallace were married, Wallace's ex-wife constantly called the house, called Donna names when she answered, and left harassing messages on the answering machine. The calls became so disturbing that Donna filed police reports and eventually blocked all the numbers from where the ex-wife could call into the house. One day, the ex-wife assaulted Donna and Donna and Wallace's toddler son was hit in the crossfire. Wallace did not do much to protect Donna and gave little encouragement for Donna to file charges.

It is good for a woman to know as much as possible about the mothers of a man's children.

If the children's mothers are not happy campers and are still harboring ill feelings towards him, those mothers will try to bring that unhappiness into the father's camp and into the father's woman's life.

Other questions to ask about the children's mothers:

- **How does he get along with each of the kids' momma (yesterday and today)?**

- **What are the personality, behavior, marital or relationship status and lifestyle of each child's momma (yesterday and today)?**

Having an idea about how a man gets along with his children's mother(s) as well as knowing what the mother's particular behavioral history has been can give a woman somewhat of a gauge on how much drama could surface.

Pay attention to the presence of drama he allows in his life and recognize his judgment of character.

It is of the utmost importance to know if he stands up and quickly puts an end to drama from his children's mother(s). If he tolerates hostile, disrespectful behavior from the mother(s), then that should be a dealbreaker because he may allow that same drama to come into your life.

If the children's mother(s) are happy in their own lives with a financially stable lifestyle and healthy relationships of their own, hopefully the mother(s) would be less likely to cause drama to the father and his household. This is probable – not necessarily a guarantee.

Note: Pay attention to how he relates to his children's mothers. If it is too friendly, there may still be some sort of relationship going on other than parenthood.

What are the custodial arrangements for each child, if any?

Give much thought on if you are willing to help raise another woman's child in your home.

If the man has joint custody of a child whose mother has demonstrated ill feelings, you must strongly consider the ramifications that will be introduced into your life.

How much is he paying for child support payments for each child, if any?

Child support payments that a man must pay means there is less money he has to come into a household. Sometimes a man needs financial assistance from the woman in his life due to his child support obligations. Some women have a problem with this and some women do not.

Be true to yourself to determine what you are willing to do and not willing to do, then stick to that decision.

What is the amount of child support arrearages he has yet to pay for each child, if any?

Income tax refunds, lump sum payouts, and other income are all subject to garnishment for child support arrearages. This is a strong consideration for a woman to take before co-mingling finances with someone who has child support arrearages.

What is the possibility of him having kids he did not know about popping up later?

A man may mention this voluntarily in conversation while sharing stories about his past. If a woman listens closely enough, she would be able to determine how possible it could very well be that he has children whom he does not know exist.

His Childhood

Gina grew up in an affluent suburb and Bradley grew up in public housing in a neighborhood known for having a high crime rate. Gina grew up with her mother and father and Bradley grew up in a single-family household. Gina did not think one way or the other about how Bradley grew up. Gina eventually fell in love with Bradley. When Bradley and Gina got married, Gina's family helped get them started - but unbeknownst to everybody else, Bradley resented it. Little by little, Bradley's jealousy about Gina's family began to grow. Gina was tired of receiving food stamps and other welfare benefits and wanted to begin building a lifestyle to which she was accustomed. Bradley told Gina's mother that Gina was overly ambitious to think that the lifestyle she wanted could be created overnight. Gina's credit went down the drain, all of the utilities were turned off, and they were both headed to eviction court. Gina wound up back home with her parents and Bradley went to live with his mother. Gina saved up some money and got a new apartment. Bradley moved in. When Gina got tired of Bradley stealing money from her, she moved out one day when Bradley was gone for the day and filed for divorce.

Childhood experiences shape an adult's approach and outlook to life and also shape how he or she treats others.

Learning about his childhood allows you to get some indication about where he is from, where he is coming from, and what is his determination and ambition level.

Who were his childhood friends? Is he still in touch with them?

Learn about the types of friends a man made during his youth. Take note if he ventured beyond school and the neighborhood when he developed his friendships.

What cities, states, or countries did he live in growing up?

A man who grew up living in different places does not necessarily mean that he had an unstable childhood. Living in different places could have allowed him to learn how to cultivate relationships with different people and how to adapt in an ever-changing situation. If his parents were in the military or worked in corporate America - that could explain the various opportunities he had to experience different cultures and learn many things. However, if he moved every three months due to evictions or poor choices that his parents or guardians took, that is an indication of instability.

Other questions to ask about youthful experiences

- **Did he grow up in a house, apartment, condo, or low-income housing?**

- **What games did he play outside?**

- **How did he get to school - walk, bike, school bus, city bus, ride by family or friend?**

- **What extracurricular activities was he in?**

- **What were his after-school personal activities?**

- **What did he do during the summer?**

- **What did he do on weekends growing up?**

- **What were his favorite TV shows?**

- **How was he punished or grounded?**

- **What vacations did his family take while growing up?**

- **Did his family move around a lot or did he just live in one neighborhood his entire childhood?**

His Family

From where did his family originate (on his mother's and father's side)? In what cities, states, or countries does his kin on both sides currently live?

As small as this world is, there needs to be lengthy conversations about family ties. Imagine how disappointing, shocking, or embarrassing it is for a couple to find out that they are blood relatives after having been intimate or having children.

Knowing more about a man's family's origin gives a richer knowledge about the man you are inviting into to your life.

What are or were his parents' or guardian's names?

This is general discussion. However, if a woman is contemplating building a future and a family with a man, she should begin building a mental family tree.

How old are his parents or guardians and where are their hometowns?

Again, this is just more information to learn about the man who you are inviting into your life.

What kind of role model were his mother and father?

If his mother had men over all the time around him and/or in and out of her bed when he was young, that may have an affect on how he views a woman as well as his expectations on how she should or should not be and act. If his mother was a saint, then he may think that no woman could hold a candle to his mother. If his father was the epitome of a gentleman, then he may strive to walk in that same manner or he may feel he may not ever live up to the level. If his father was a rolling stone or never in the picture, then it is possible he may approach committed relationships and household settings in the same manner.

What is and/or was his relationship with his mother? What is and/or was his relationship with his father?

A child's relationship with a parent, from childhood to old age, is the foundation of how that child will relate to men and women, especially in their personal relationships. If a man has issues with his mother, then he may have issues with women in general. If a man grew up without a father, he could either be an absentee father in his own children's lives or a man who vows to always be in his children's life no matter what.

How did his parents/guardians get along with each other? Was his home a peaceful home or was there continuous fighting or violence in the household?

Find out what he witnessed as a child when it came to his parents relating to each other.

Other parent/guardian related questions

- **Were his parents ever married to each other? If not, why weren't they?**

- **Did either of his parents cheat on the other?**

- **Were his parents ever divorced - how many times - why did they get divorced?**

- **Had his parents ever divorced then remarried each other?**

- **Did his parents ever marry someone else - how many marriages? How did those subsequent marriages wind up?**

- **What did his parents/guardians do for a living?**

Are his parents or childhood guardians alive?

If his parents are alive, pay attention to how involved he is in their lives and how involved they are in his life. One extreme could be too involved and the other extreme could be as if they never existed. Find out if there is a happy medium and if there is not, learn as to why.

Are there any family criminal histories?

Some people may have a predisposition for certain behaviors. It is possible that someone in his family, including his children, may open a door of drama into his life in any number of ways.

Was he born or adopted into the family?

Beatrice and Gary married and had three beautiful children. When the oldest became a teenager, Gary began having muscle control issues. Eventually, Gary was diagnosed with a debilitating neurological disease. The doctor told Gary that the disease was generally hereditary. When Gary told his parents what the doctor said and asked as to whom else in the family had the disease, his parents told him that he was adopted. Gary was well into his 40s. Gary succumbed to the disease after a lengthy stay in the nursing home. Soon after, one by one, Gary and Beatrice's three children began showing signs of the same disease. All three children went through the same pattern of deterioration as their father and passed away.

Genetics play a big part in an individual's make-up and future. However, there is no guarantee of even a grown man knowing his true biological background if the adoptive parents swore to take the truth to their graves while everyone else around took the same oath.

What are the names, ages, locations, and birthdates of all of his siblings? Are the siblings full, half, step, fostered, or adopted? What is his relationship with each sibling?

No amount of information is too much when learning about a man's family. This bit of information sheds a little light on if his family is a close-knit family or if members in his family have little to no contact with each other.

His Money

Victoria and Walter decided to purchase a home. When it came time to apply for a mortgage loan, Walter had no credit history and his annual income was not as high as Victoria's income. Walter just started a new job. Victoria had great credit and had been on her job for almost 10 years. The home was titled in both Victoria and Walter's names. Victoria was the primary applicant.

Steph and Julian had been together for a year and decided to rent a home together. They fell in love with a home and submitted an application. They both provided all the information and verification as requested and Steph just knew they had the home. The property manager told Steph and Julian that their application was denied due to eviction filings and a recent bankruptcy. Steph had good credit, never filed bankruptcy and always paid her rent on time. Steph did not know Julian had filed bankruptcy and had been evicted four times until that day.

If a woman has taken the time to get herself together financially, then she owes it to herself to know fully a man's financial history, money management patterns, current assets, debts, and child support obligations/arrearages.

If you are contemplating co-mingling your finances and partnering up with a man who will be involved in providing shelter over you and your family's head, you must address this topic head-on.

If a man wants to tiptoe around this subject, then tiptoe backwards from this relationship. Finance is one of the top reasons for relationship troubles or relationships ending. There is no better time than the beginning to understand a potential companion's financial status.

Prior to asking financial related questions to a man, an intelligent woman has already answered these questions for herself and has already established firm financial footing with financial goals, resources, and action plans in place. If she knows where she is and where she wants to be, then she will automatically know where he needs to be if he is to be with her.

A mature, financially healthy, and intelligent man WILL have the answers to these questions.

The time for you to find out these things is during early conversations and definitely BEFORE submitting any type of joint application.

What is his current credit score?

No person should be talking to another person if they do not know their credit score. Anyone who does not know their credit score, needs to sit at home by themselves and find out because everything from insurance rates to mortgage and auto loans are dictated by a credit score.

If you have worked to have good credit, then you need to co-mingle your money with someone who also had good credit.

What is his past credit history?

If it is excellent, gain some tips. If it is bad, then find out what he is doing right now about it.

What are his current credit practices now?

Take the time to see if he pays by cash or check. If he flips out a credit card all of the time, and that is a credit card not a debit card, then credit is a major component in his day-to-day spending.

Some people use credit cards for financial record management. If he is able to pay off the balances every month, then he is wise when it comes to credit utilization.

If you hear him making payment arrangements or receiving debt collection calls, take note. That is a red flag.

What is his financial history?

Divorce, sickness, and other unforeseen circumstances can zap a person's financial position even when someone believes they followed the proper steps to secure their finances. However, a pattern of bad habits and carelessness is another story, so listen carefully to that story. Although unforeseen circumstances are legitimate, be sure you do not allow those circumstances to be his excuses — especially if those matters happened a decade or so ago.

What is his bankruptcy history?

Bankruptcy can be the result of anything out of someone's control as long as it is not the method of debt management every 7 plus years while going back and forth between Chapter 7 and Chapter 13.

What is his residential history - owned or rented, in own name or in others' i.e. family, partner, spouse?

A man who is able to obtain a home in his name with his own money and financial credentials is an ideal man. He has demonstrated that he can secure and maintain property on his own without the financial assistance or co-signature of another.

An intelligent woman deserves a man who can handle financial business without needing her assistance, even if she is willing or able to help.

What is his judgment history?

Unsettled judgments for back taxes, medical bills, or consumer debt can wreak havoc on a person's credit history. If a person has unsatisfied judgments, he or she may find it difficult to obtain certification or licensing in regulated industries such as finance or real estate.

A financially fit woman would want to be involved with a man who has no unpaid judgments.

What are his current debt balances?

Low debt balances are manageable if an easy payment plan has been established. However, if he has debt balances that are so high that it would require bankruptcy to escape, then he is still working on getting his finances in order.

What are his money saving practices?

A man who has established his retirement funds, money market accounts, passbook savings accounts, and so on, is on the right track and serious about his financial status.

Established women spend time with established men.

What were the spending habits of his parents or guardians growing up?

Sometimes the spending patterns of the adults carry on to the children in the household. If his parents or guardians were careless regarding money matters, either he learned to do better with money management or he adopted their style of spending.

It is up to you to pay attention to his spending patterns.

Other Financial Related Questions

- **What are his money spending priorities, habits, patterns?**
- **What was his household income when growing up?**
- **What were his money beliefs a few years ago?**
- **What are his money beliefs today?**
- **What is a ballpark figure of his current savings balance?**
- **What are his financial goals?**
- **What are his asset goals? Are there mutual funds, stocks and bonds, real estate investment, etc?**

Does he have a life insurance policy in place?

If a man has children, he should have a life insurance policy - unless he has been denied due to health and age.

The rule of thumb is that the policy amount is 10 times the amount of his current income. No man should be without a life insurance policy while expecting his parents or family to bear the cost of his final expenses.

Pay attention to how he looks out for his children's financial needs and best interests.

Does he have a current Last Will and Testament in existence?

A Last Will and Testament is a sign of financial maturity and sensitivity to handling matters while having things in order for his loved ones.

A man, especially a man with children, should have this document already in place and updated annually.

Does he have a Heath Care POA and/or a Living Will?

A man who has his Health Care Directive and/or a Living Will in place shows that he has immense financial maturity. It also shows that he gave great thought to communicate his wishes throughout all aspects of his life should a day came where he could not convey his wishes himself.

His Profession

How does he make his money today?

When Eileen met Dustin he always had a roll of bills in his pocket. Dustin had a good job working for a manufacturing company and had been there for several months. Somewhere along the line, Dustin stopped working at the manufacturing company and started working at various places through an employment agency. Eileen allowed the roll of bills in Dustin's pocket sway her into thinking that he was a wealthy man and had it all together.

Eileen never took into consideration that Dustin was on public transportation, only wore work clothes, and lived with family members.

What is his work history?

- **Has he had two or three long-term positions or ten to fifteen short-term opportunities?**

- **Is there a pattern of being fired frequently or does he leave voluntarily?**

- **If he left voluntarily was it because of a better opportunity or just because he did not like the job?**

- **If he had many jobs in the last few years was it attributed to the economy, personal circumstances, or just an inability to hold a job?**

Is he a day hustler or a serious entrepreneur?

There is a difference between someone who is an entrepreneur and someone who is a day-to-day hustler. An entrepreneur takes the time to develop a business operation or acquire existing operations to add to his business portfolio. A day-to-day hustler is someone who gets contracted to work for the day doing anything from odd jobs to employment agencies to self-employment initiatives.

One type of role is no better or worse than the other. Both, the hustler and the entrepreneur can keep food on the table and a roof over a head. There may be a slight risk of instability with these roles, but of course, nothing is guaranteed – even a full time, good paying job.

Ask yourself again if you are comfortable with a man who has decided not to earn his living as an employee.

Does he have any professional degrees or licenses?

A man who has degrees or licenses merely shows his discipline to achieve higher education only. His academic achievements will not gauge if he would be a compatible or great companion.

If you are interested in higher learning, then most likely a man interested in the same would be ideal.

Does he have a current resume?

Usually, individuals who are in the workforce are interested in obtaining better and greater opportunities. If the man is ambitious, it would be interesting if he has a current resume available for opportunities that present themselves at any time.

What is his ultimate dream job?

Is he working toward that dream or just letting each day come and go to see what will happen next?

What is his ultimate dream profession?

Again, is he working toward that dream?

Has he ever served in the military?

What branch, how long, highest rank achieved, honorable or dishonorable discharge? If dishonorable discharge, why?

Is his current profession legal, ethical, or morally right?

Ideally, an intelligent single woman is only interested in a man whose career will not have law enforcement officials or unhappy rivals knocking on the door at any given time.

Your highest priority is to continually protect your household, you, and your family's life from drama brought on by someone else's actions.

His Health

What are his biological family health histories for both sides - auto immune ailments, neurological ailments, cardiology, oncology, respiratory, allergies, surgical procedures, digestive, diabetes, hypertension, glaucoma, hearing loss, blindness, any other illnesses or diseases, etc.?

Back to Beatrice and Gary. Beatrice buried not her only husband but her three children from a genetic neurological disease.

This is an area about a companion where many men and women do not know about until decades later when conditions begin to develop.

If a person does not know their biological family health histories on both sides, it could prove to be a disadvantage if treatment for certain health concerns is needed. Although treatment would go forth, healthcare professionals appreciate biological family health histories to rule out possible allergic reactions.

What is his personal health history - auto immune ailments, neurological ailments, allergies, cardiology, oncology, respiratory, surgical procedures, digestive, diabetes, hypertension, glaucoma, hearing loss, blindness, any other illnesses or diseases, injuries, etc.?

These are things to know if spending time with someone because who knows when there may be a medical emergency and you are the only one around.

Secondly, some health conditions are genetic. Knowing some of these things beforehand can provide opportunity to establish preventative measures before conditions worsen as well as begin dialogue with the children regarding healthier eating habits and historical health information.

What is his surgery/operations/hospitalization history?

This type of question could never be an invasion of privacy ESPECIALLY if a woman is entertaining having a physical relationship with a man.

Is he a current organ donor?

This is another general question to ask.

Is there any sterility?

If a woman who wishes to have children meets a man who is sterile, then both the man and the woman need to have a planned parenthood discussion in the very beginning to discuss:

- Options for treatment

- Adoption or foster care options

- A decision to continue or to stop seeing each other

Again, does he have current Health Care Power of Attorney/Living Will documents in existence?

A responsible adult, married or single, children or not, should have a Health Care Power of Attorney and Living Will documents.

Does he exercise and practice good eating habits?

Do you wish to be involved with a man who practices healthy habits or with a man who just lives day to day with no concern about his weight, eating habits, and/or general health?

Addictions and Mental Health

What are his family drug or alcoholism histories? Is there any specific personal and family drug use history - what type, how often?

Learn more about the people who could or will potentially be around you, your family, and your home.

Does he have any personal history of drug or alcoholism?

If there is any history of drug use or alcoholism, learn the details and timeline. Find out if there is any current use or find out how long sobriety has been in place.

What is his family's mental health history - depression, anxiety, phobias, etc.?

Some mental health conditions are hereditary and could not only pass down to the man, but to his children as well. This is not to say that just because someone in the family has had a mental health condition that it would automatically be the case for everyone in the family including the children.

However, if you are planning to have children, information about his family's medical and mental health history is crucial.

Other mental health questions

- Is he or any members of his family currently under medical care and/or receiving medications to treat any mental or behavioral health disorders or diseases?

- What is his personal mental health history - depression, anxiety, phobias, etc.?

- What is his family's behavioral health history - Obsessive-compulsive disorder, schizophrenia, bipolar?

- **What is his personal behavioral health history - Obsessive-compulsive disorder, schizophrenia, bipolar?**

- **Is there any current drug use now? What type, how often?**

- **How often does he take a drink - social, hardly ever, or every day?**

This is the kind of information that needs to be learned AFTER a woman has taken her dealmaker and dealbreaker inventory.

The ideal time to decide to enter into a relationship with someone who currently has a substance abuse or mental health condition is in the beginning when you have already done your soul searching to determine what you could or absolutely could not be a part of – what you can handle and what you definitely could not handle.

It is not selfish to decide a man's current mental health, drug use, or alcoholism is too much to handle and to walk away. Your decision must be fair to and is based upon your current capabilities and to your current household and family obligations/needs.

Anyone can develop a mental health or substance abuse problem after a relationship has been established. You can cross that bridge if it ever comes. The key at this point is to recognize what is currently on the table and what you are willing to invite in your life.

Sexual Health

The spread of sexually transmitted infections or diseases including HIV/AIDs continues. The number one way to avoid contracting a sexually transmitted disease or infection is to practice abstinence. Other than that, no matter how well a woman knows a man, she could never be 100% sure that he does not have any sexually transmitted conditions.

Many people do not know they have been affected by a sexually transmitted disease, as all infections do not produce symptoms. Sometimes people find out that they have a sexually transmitted infection while being treated or screened for another health condition.

Even if a woman and a man has a mature conversation about their sexual history, it does not mean that one or the other will divulge the truth about their sexual history because he or she may not want to scare off the other.

Second to abstinence or celibacy, testing for a disease with a partner prior to sexual intimacy could minimize the risk of contracting a sexually transmitted infection or disease – if enough time has elapsed for the condition to be detected.

Trust is the number one factor when it comes to sexual engagement.

If there is any inkling of doubt, trust your woman's intuition and discernment and cease any sexual contact – because unless you have a man under 24-hour surveillance, there is nothing else to ensure his monogamy.

Julie and Frederick were married for almost three years. Two years after the divorce, Julie decided to start dating again and went to the gynecologist to get birth control. Julie learned she had chlamydia. For as long as five years, Julie had a condition that causes destruction to fallopian tubes and/or fertility issues.

Hillary had been seeing Victor for about three years and they had always talked about getting married. Hillary had settled with Victor because her only focus was getting married while she continued to ignore their incompatibility. Hillary contracted genital herpes from Victor. Genital herpes is incurable and only shows signs of infection during outbreaks. Genital herpes sores look like one or more blisters on or around the genitals, rectum, or mouth. The blisters break and become painful sores that may take weeks to heal. Sometimes flu-like symptoms are experienced during an outbreak. (Source about genital herpes: www.cdc.gov)

Leslie and Hector had been seeing each other for a year or so. However, Hector was promiscuous, engaged in orgies, and was bi-sexual. Hector contracted HIV. Leslie did not learn that she could possibly be infected until Hector became ill as his condition progressed from HIV to AIDS. Unfortunately, Leslie tested HIV positive. Leslie was five months pregnant.

What are his feelings about using a condom?

Since the invention of condoms, men today still tell women that a condom takes away their sensation and enjoyment of making love. Women still today buy that story.

There is not enough sensation in the world where you owe it to a man to jeopardize your health and life. If you decide that you are ready for intimacy, you must stay caught up in your health, your future, and that of which for your family. Do not get caught up in a moment that will definitely turn out to be brief and temporarily pleasurable – and is not promised that it would be all that pleasurable.

Your life and future is much more valuable than "feeling good" or achieving an orgasm – either for him or for you.

What if he beats you to climax – then what? Was it worth the risk? Unprotected sex will never be worth the risk.

What are his feelings about using birth control?

If you know that you are not in a committed relationship then the question of using birth control is a mute point. You should not be intimate with him at all unless you are willing to contract a sexual disease and able to care for a child on your own.

Relationships that began on promises of being together forever end every day.

If speaking about the future as a married couple, then this would be the time to discuss birth control methods but in the interim, abstinence, celibacy, or a condom with another type of birth control is the order of the day.

What are his past STD test results? What are his current STD/HIV test results?

YOUR life depends on these types of discussions. How he responds to your questions will give you some indication on how serious he takes his own sexual health.

The best way to get these answers is to get tested together.

Sexual Behavior

Sheila and Cleo saw each other for two years before they got married. Before they were married, Sheila asked Cleo to pick up her teenage daughter from her rehearsal and bring the daughter up to Sheila's job. Cleo's mother volunteered to come along. A short time later, Cleo's mother told Sheila that the reason why she picked Sheila's daughter up and brought her to the job was because one time, a woman that Cleo had been seeing said that Cleo was making inappropriate jesters around the woman's daughter and she thought it would be better not for Cleo to be placed in that position.

After Sheila and Cleo settled into their new home after two years of marriage, Sheila was looking through the search history for something on the computer and came across disturbing pictures of odd-looking people in various sexual poses. She could not tell if they were men or women. Sheila figured it was Cleo because they had argued before about Cleo spending money on pornographic websites. Sheila knew that Cleo enjoyed pornographic videos but thought that would stop once they got married. Later, Sheila noticed that when she and Cleo were out, he would point out individuals who looked like women that were actually men. When Sheila took a closer look, she realized he was right. Sheila started wondering how he could tell so quickly and wondered why it intrigued him so. Then Sheila thought back to the disturbing images on the computer.

Years after the divorce, an investigative officer from the county Family Services called Sheila to inform her that Cleo was under investigation for sexually molesting a child - his daughter from a previous relationship. The investigative officer asked Sheila to come down and bring her young daughter in for questioning. Years later, Sheila's daughters gave indication that they were sexually molested by Cleo when they were younger.

Whenever children are involved, it is a mother's responsibility to probe, observe, and never doubt the sexual preferences, fetishes, or fantasies that a man is capable of having - as he may carry out those desires with the most vulnerable individuals who are close at hand. A woman must never underestimate what a man is capable of doing and must never be confident on what a man will or will not do.

You owe the most vulnerable in your household to keep your ears and eyes wide open when it comes to all dialogue and interaction with not just you, but with the ones you love.

Even more important, a woman must have an open, clear, uninhibited communication channel with her children. Children must know that they can come to their mother even if they were threatened not to do so. Your children must know that their relationship with you is more important to you than the relationship that you have with any man – including their father. A good mother will make that message loud and clear to her children.

Discussing sexual behavior, desires, and preferences with a man should be in length, should be effortless, and must be done in a mature, non-defensive manner. If the man gives you pushback or any hint of feeling insulted, steer clear from placing your health and the welfare of your children in the hands of someone disinterested, ego-driven, and immature to have the discussion.

Any man who cannot understand your concern about your sexual health and the welfare of your children is not mature enough to have a relationship with you.

Be sure to search the name, date of birth, and address of every man you begin to talk to or date in criminal and sexual offender records.

If you do not find any records in those databases, it does not mean he is not capable of committing any sex crimes. Any man is capable. No records may mean he may not have been caught as yet.

Cleo and Sheila were very active in community affairs. Cleo would often time point to a little girl and tell Sheila how cute that little girl was. Sheila would agree and move on thinking nothing more about it.

When the allegations and accusations came out about Cleo molesting a young girl, then Sheila recalled the times Cleo pointed out "cute" little girls.

The time to pay attention to what is said, how often it is said, and when it is said, is at all times.

Cleo inadvertently let Sheila know about his attraction to little girls the whole time.

What is his current sexual skill level?

This is not to learn if he can work it in the bedroom. This is to determine that if he is advanced, it may be because he has had a lot of practice. There are ways to find out without actually becoming physical. What a man says and his mannerism can give indication.

**A lot of practice possibly means
a history with a lot of sexual partners.**

How many sexual partners has he had to date?

You could never ask this question enough times. Quite naturally, the more partners, the greater the risk in the transference of a sexually transmitted infection. However, all it takes is his having one unprotected sexual encounter.

What are his feelings about monogamy? What are his feelings about promiscuity?

As mentioned before, a woman has a gut instinct. No matter how a man may answer the question - either saying what he thinks the woman wants to hear or saying what is true feelings are about, her gut will tell her immediately if his answer jives or not. Many women choose to ignore bad feelings and shake them off. That choice can prove to be costly.

What are his feelings about pornography?

Sheila did not think much about Cleo's interest in pornography, until it continued on into the marriage.

A woman needs to make it up in her mind if she is okay with her sexual companion watching pornography on a regular basis. Some women enjoy watching pornography with their sexual partner. Some women think that the man in their life should not need pornography if she is giving the man what he wants...so she believes.

Determine if his watching pornography is or is not okay with you.

What are his sexual expectations?

If a woman is contemplating a long-term relationship with a man, then she needs to know what he expects from her as his sexual companion. If she does not feel she can deliver, then she should be true to herself and either try to meet those sexual expectations or let it be known that she believes she may not able to do so.

A man who is not sexually satisfied will go elsewhere to find someone who can and will satisfy him. Where there is promiscuity, there is risk to contract a sexually transmitted disease.

What are his sexual energy/stamina/frequency desires?

If a man wants to go all day everyday, then his sexual partner should want and be willing to do the same.

Since intimacy should be a two-way street, a woman's desires must be matched as well.

If you want frequent sexual encounters that will go all night long, your sexual partner should be able to meet that desire.

When was the last time he was sexually intimate with

someone?

Again, be sure that enough time has passed from his last sexual encounter for any STDs to show up. Probe further about the behavior of his last sexual partner to find out if he or she was promiscuous.

Remember, sleeping with one person is sleeping with everybody they have slept with and everybody those people have slept with, and so on.

Is he currently sexually intimate with someone?

Realistically, a man is not going to just come out and say that he is sleeping with someone else while trying to get something going with you.

A man may have somebody on the side for sexual gratification throughout the entire time you are involved with him.

This is another example to pay attention to not what only he says, but what he does. Pay attention to his communication and dating patterns with you. If something seems fishy, then it means that something fishy is going on.

What are his sexual fantasies?   What are his sexual fetishes?

If a man is into threesomes and you are not, then that will be a problem. There may be some sexual fantasies you may not wish to fulfill.

This area uncovers two things:

1. This exposes what he may be into and into what you may not be willing to indulge.
2. If you pay close attention, you may uncover potential risks to you and your children.

While disagreements about money cause break-ups, so do disagreements about sexual activities.

When was his first time? How old was he?

This is a general question to ask.

What is his sexual preference - Heterosexual, homosexual or bisexual?

You will just have to figure out some of this on your own. There are men who would never disclose being homosexual or bi-sexual.

Follow your gut instinct.

What are his feelings about swinging?

If he shares interest in having an open relationship, then he has sounded the alarm that you may be in an open relationship – whether you want to or not. If he contracts anything, you are at risk to contract the disease as well if you make the decision to be sexually involved with him.

His Character

What is his current driving record? Does he have a history of any DUIs or suspended licenses?

Reckless behavior in one area can show up to be reckless in another area. If a woman is contemplating on inviting a man into her world, unnecessary costs like court fines and license reinstatement costs are not in the order toward financial stability.

More importantly, a woman who is conscious about safety and health does not have her family or herself in a vehicle driven by someone who has demonstrated a disregard for his safety and the safety of others.

Other criminal related questions

- **Does he have a criminal record?**

- **Has he ever been convicted of anything?**

- **Has he ever served any jail time?**

- **Has he ever been on probation?**

- **Is he currently on parole or recently released from a correctional institution?**

People do things that they greatly regret later when they are young or if pushed into a dire situation. However, there should not be a current pattern of criminal activity on any level. Some men are open to sharing their criminal past and some keep it secret out of fear of rejection.

Most criminal court records can be researched online while some correctional institutions only give history on those who are currently serving time. The key is not to condemn because of a criminal record. The focus is on what steps he has taken to turn his life around.

Again, pay attention on what a man does to back-up what he says he is doing.

Recreation related questions

- **Would he like to take a cross-country road trip or would he rather fly directly to his specific destination?**

- **What other things would he like to do i.e. take a cruise, skydiving, scuba diving, bungee jumping, skiing, taking a continental train trip, touring a museum, walking through a park, fishing at the lake, etc.?**

This is where compatibility is important. Couples who have been together for a great number of decades say that what has kept them together was doing things together that they BOTH enjoyed.

The most important component for your relationship is to be able to enjoy each other's company outside of the bedroom.

Lifetime companionship has a longer duration then sexual libido or ability.

What are his hobbies?

A woman does not have to share every hobby that a man does and vice versa. This is pretty much just a topic of general discussion.

However, for example, if he likes to go scuba diving and you do not know how to swim, then you will either need to learn how to swim or sit on the boat in a life jacket until he comes back up to the surface.

What outside activities does he like to do?

Again, this is another general discussion topic.

What inside activities does he like to do?

If a woman is a homebody but the man likes to go out a lot to eat or have fun with friends every night, then the both of them will have to either compromise or agree that they are not compatible in this particular area.

Spirituality/Religion

People argue about religion and spirituality. There is little peace when two are of uneven yoke in spiritual beliefs and religious practices unless there is an utmost of mutual respect and agreement. If there is not a level of grand respect, then there is great potential for one to debate that his or hers spiritual beliefs and religious practices are the only and right way.

This does not mean that a woman must already have an established spiritual belief or religious practice because she may not have discovered something in that realm where she is most comfortable. The man may actually introduce a spiritual belief or practice that changes her life for the better.

However, if you have an established spiritual belief or religious practice, make the decision to either be open to new spiritual and religious ideas or closed so you will not be swayed from your beliefs.

All religions believe in a higher being. The difference is that each religion calls the higher being a different name and has their own interpretation about the higher being's meaning, purpose, and dominion along with their own doctrine and literature to support their beliefs.

You will need to decide where you would be most comfortable regarding you and his religious practices and spiritual beliefs.

What religion did he practice while growing up?

This is a general discussion topic.

What was he taught as far as men and women relations?

If he was raised up in the church, it does not necessarily mean that he has the same beliefs today as an adult. Many women believe that because a man comes from a "God-fearing, church-going" family, that he will make a good companion and an excellent husband.

On the contrary, depending on what he was taught, he may feel that women are subservient and have no say in any matters. As far as he is concerned, women are no more than children and must be treated as such.

How does he feel about women leadership at his place of worship?

A woman who feels she has been called to minister in leadership needs to know if the man in her world will be supportive of that decision.

You have no time to ever be in a situation where your significant other is not supportive in your spiritual beliefs - especially if and when you feel guided to be a voice to spread a message.

Has he felt he has been called to be a leader in spiritual or religious teachings?

This is a very important topic to discuss because if a man is a leader in a place of worship, it will be expected that his companion is a visible supportive partner.

You need to determine if you are willing and ready to assume that role.

Other religion/spiritual related questions

- **Does he believe in God or is he agnostic, an atheist, or a devil/satanic worshipper?**

- **If he believes in God, is it the same God that you believe in?**

- **What are his feelings about religion?**

- **What are his feelings about spirituality?**

- **What religion does he practice today?**

- **What are his worship practices - home, church, synagogue, mosque, etc.?**

- **How often does he go to a place of worship - daily, weekly, monthly, quarterly, or once a year? If weekly or monthly, is he active in any ministry? If so, how active?**

- **Does he give charitable donations regularly? If yes, what organizations or charities does he support?**

- Is he open to worshipping with you or elsewhere upon invitation?

- Has he invited you to his place of worship?

- If you both have your own places of worship, how and where would you both worship after marriage?

Education

Find out where he has come from and where he would like to go. Continuous education is a pathway to growth. Although a man with a doctorate does not prove that he is better than a man whose highest education is sixth grade, the man with the doctorate has demonstrated perseverance in furthering his education.

Higher education is not for everybody as many successful people have never stepped foot into a college. Using a person's education history as a judgment tool tells you very little about his intelligence. However, learning about his education history and goals gives you another opportunity to know him better and to determine if you both share similar viewpoints about education.

Education/training related questions

- **What schools did he attend - grade school, middle school, high school diploma or GED?**

- **What colleges did he attend? What were the courses?**

- **Has he had any vocational training?**

- **What was the last level of education he received?**

- **Does he have any plans for future education? If so, when?**

- **What is his ongoing education preference for college, vocational/trade, online, etc.?**

- **What are his beliefs about public or private education?**

- **What are his beliefs about college education and various types of institutions (Jewish, Catholic, Christian, Historically Black Colleges, Ivy League)?**

Dreams and Aspirations - What Does He Want Out of Life?

Deena is a social worker and dreams of starting a non-profit organization to help at-risk youth gain interview and job skills. Deena wants to make a difference in not only the children's lives but also in the children's households.

Leonard is content in his current career as a school bus driver. Leonard is not trying to do anything else for the rest of the day until it is time to pull the bus out the next morning.

Deena works on her plans and has meetings to make the non-profit organization a reality. Leonard does not attend any of the meetings and oftentimes ask Deena why is she continually trying to save the world. If Deena does not stick to her dreams, she could easily be discouraged by Leonard's point of view, thus, leaving one less program to make a difference in a child's life.

A couple can grow together and stay together because of mutual spiritual beliefs or shared recreational activities. A couple on the same page about aspirations and dreams could prove to be a powerful couple together.

Other aspiration/dream related questions

- **Is he a dreamer?**
- **What is his dream home?**
- **What is his dream car?**
- **What were his dreams when he was a kid?**
- **What were his dreams as a teenager?**
- **What is his dream vacation?**
- **Where has he ever dreamt about living?**
- **What are his other dreams or aspirations?**
- **What are his goals in making a difference in his neighborhood or in society?**

Emotional/Support Needs

Turning the tables for just a moment, ask yourself the following questions:

- **Do I require frequent affection or attention or do I require time and space alone?**

- **When I go to a function whether at church, to one of my children's school related event, or some other type of function, do I expect my significant other to join me?**

April is very affectionate and loves to be held. Norman, on the other hand, believes a peck on the kiss and a hug here and there should suffice about his affection toward April. April needs to be honest with herself regarding her expectations of having abundant affection and companionship. If she does not, then she will be very miserable in a relationship with Norman.

Natalie is very independent and is not the touchy feely type. Kirk, on the other hand, wants to kiss and hug on Natalie every chance he gets. Eventually, Natalie is going to grow tired of Kirk, feel smothered, and begin pushing Kirk away.

Sophie hates to go to any function alone. Aaron would rather die than go to a social event. Sophie and Aaron will not be compatible in this regard.

What is in it for you?

As it has been said before, a relationship is a two-way street. Both parties need to feel that they are receiving what they need, desire, and reasonably expect from the other.

You must not only give your contribution to the relationship, but you must absolutely ensure that you are receiving what you need out of the relationship.

Additional questions to ask yourself especially as some time has passed

- **Is he supportive of my dreams, ideals, and/or decisions objectively or does he mock or belittle them?**

- **Does he have female friends that he mentioned but I have yet to meet or with whom I have yet to have any interactions?**

If you are uncomfortable with any of the honest answers that you give yourself to these questions, use that discomfort to move yourself into a respectful, peaceful, healthy, and happy relationship.

If a man is not the one, then he is simply just not the one.

SKELETONS IN THE CLOSET

The skeletons in the closet are the things that will not enter into a conversation randomly. The skeletons are the deep seeded experiences that most would rather take to their grave than share with anyone.

Although those skeletons are private, some skeletons are necessary to know. You will not be able to force any information out of anyone. But the topics in this section can be discussed while explored delicately.

Has he ever been sexually molested, sodomized, or raped? If so, by whom, how often, and at what age?

Many men who have been sexually molested, sodomized, or raped prefer to carry that experience to their graves. Those types of experiences may and most likely affect a man's sexual preferences, desires, and expectations.

A man who has experienced such trauma may:

- Be confused about their sexuality and sexual preferences

- Have an enormous and insatiable appetite for sex including pornography and multiple sexual partners which would cause infidelity while in a relationship

- Sexually molest, sodomize, or rape others regardless of age and/or gender

- Find it difficult to have a healthy sexual relationship with a woman

Other skeleton-type related questions include:

- Has he ever been involved in an incestuous relationship?

- Has he ever witnessed a heinous act of crime or abuse?

- Has he ever committed a heinous act of crime or abuse?

COMPATIBILITY AND COMMITMENT

Compatibility

Determining compatibility is quite simple. Take what you have learned and what you believe to be valid and compare it with what you must have in a relationship to see if there is compatibility.

At the end of the day and what is most important is compatibility. Not if a man looks the part or if momma, daddy, family, or friends will approve. Compatibility is a personal determination. Compatibility is the foundation for peace, love, and joy. Incompatibility is the foundation for drama, animosity, and depression.

The goal of compatibility must never be compromised.

Commitment

After discovering compatibility, the next phase would be commitment.

But here is the most important cautionary note in this book. There is no commitment unless there is a conversation confirming a committed relationship.

The two major types of commitment that could be presented are:

- Sexual commitment - this type of commitment is generally short-term with the foundation of the commitment based on a physical relationship only - where both parties agree they will not be intimate with anyone else.

- Lifetime companion commitment - this type of commitment is a healthy type of relationship as long as there is mutual respect and mutual compatibility between the two.

A committed relationship is not in place unless the "commitment conversation" has taken place. A woman can be committed to a man all day long, but a man may not feel the same way, even if she "thinks" he "acts" that way.

The committed relationship discussion is when the man brings it up.

If a woman brings up the conversation regarding commitment, she is taking the winds from a man's sail. Some may say that there is nothing wrong with a woman speaking up about her feelings and what she wants. Which there is not. But men are made up of conquering and achieving. They have not conquered or achieved if the woman already brings it to him on a silver platter without him lifting a finger.

The best way that a woman can express that she is ready for a committed relationship is not through her mouth but merely by her actions.

If a woman:
- does not take crap off of a man

- does not throw her life and family obligations to the back burner to accommodate wherever or whatever a man wishes to go or do

- continues to go about her day only giving him the time of day that he has proven that he deserves

…then, she has made it pretty loud and clear the direction in which she is intending to go.

You do not have to say one word to let a man know where you stand. No matter what, if you continue to walk with a no nonsense manner, trust and believe that man knows exactly the kind of woman he is dealing with and exactly what you want – even if he acts like he does not know.

When a woman leads the commitment discussion, she may find herself in a situation where the man merely says what she wants to hear.

If a man is serious, there is no doubt he will make it known to that woman. He would not be mysterious or coy about it and he will definitely not need prodding.

If a man wants a woman, he will do exactly what he needs to do get that woman. He will do exactly what he needs to do to keep that woman.

And how he would do this? He would do it because he paid attention to the boundaries that she set forth. A real man wants a woman who has paid attention and held true to her boundaries, her dealmakers, and her dealbreakers. A real man who wants a healthy relationship would not try to change her beliefs or stand about things. If anything, it would be her beliefs, stands, and boundaries that turned him on in the first place.

TOP OF MIND

As you learn more and more about someone each day, there are certain things that you must keep top of mind:

You Must Feel Safe

If you do not feel safe or if you have the slightest hint of feeling uncomfortable around him, then you must cease being around him. A women's intuition is the radar that she was born with to protect herself, her home, and her family. There should never be a hint of feeling uncomfortable, worried, or fearful when with someone. If a woman must be alone for the rest of her life, it would be much better than being with someone whom she fears.

If a man raises his hand to you to either intimidate or to actually make one strike against you or against a family member, that must be the last time that he does it. There is no excuse for physical assault. There are not enough bad days, bad breaks, or bad moods he could ever have to warrant that kind of behavior. If it happens, make it the very last time and remove you and any family members away from that situation. There is no excuse worthy enough to continue in that position.

Stay On Your Track

If you have goals, dreams, and visions for your life prior to meeting someone, then do not set those aside to accommodate his goals, dreams, and visions.

Many may believe that a woman should set aside her desires to be subservient to the man and his vision for the hope and promise that it would be to the benefit of all. This is not exercising the right to freedom and the pursuit of happiness.

Goals, dreams, and visions do not come to those just to practice in fairyland. If you are an American, then you must always remember that you are Number One in your book and you are with one with your higher being.

You must pursue or achieve without hesitation or limitation anything that has been laid upon your heart to do.

Do Not Give Second Chances for Intentional Actions

As human beings, we are all bound to do something that may cause hurt or harm to another - intentionally and unintentionally. A woman must know her limits to giving second chances.

For instance, if a woman knows and has made it known to a man that if he decides to be intimate with another woman, the relationship that she has with him is automatically over. If the man does cheat with another woman but comes back with his reasoning on why, the woman must either stick to her guns and walk away or feel she can give a second chance.

If a man cheating on you is a dealbreaker, then it should remain as a dealbreaker. If a man stealing from you is a dealbreaker, then it should remain a dealbreaker. Assaulting you or your children is an automatic dealbreaker and should never, ever be forgiven under the gift of second chances.

Intentional actions are cheating, stealing, and assault and there could never be a good enough reason to excuse either three of these behaviors.

Be About Your Business

A woman who is busy keeping her personal and professional business in order has little time for nonsense - especially from a man. It is only then, when the sun and moon rise and set, she will be in a position to cultivate a healthy relationship with a man.

You are a special person and a special woman. If a special woman so desires to have a man in her life, that man cannot be just any man just because he came along.

A special woman MUST have a special man. The only way to know if he is special is to get to know him.

THE SIMPLE PRINCIPLE

The Simple Principle about Men and Women is as old as how long men and women have been on this earth. I wrote about this Simple Principle in **"Big Girl, Little Girl - Everything I Can Think Of Right Now To Tell You About Life, Money, Credit, Boys, Men, and Sex."** This simple principle is the very foundation of a woman's sanity and inviolability. It is the very principle that will help a woman not lose her mind, heart, body, and soul to a man -- especially to a man who does not have her best interests in mind or on his agenda.

The following excerpt about the Simple Principle is the formula to help any woman who first enters into a relationship with a man.

The Simple Principle About Men and Women

There is a principle that every female must know, understand, and operate from before cultivating a relationship with a male. This principle is ageless and it applies to the adolescent and to the old. This principle can be learned easy or it can be learned the hard way. That principle is:

- **The woman operates on intimacy and emotion.**

- **The man operates on physical attraction/gratification and the mind.**

If a woman remembers this each and every time she talks to a man, she will be approaching that conversation and relationship in the proper perspective and with realistic expectations.

- **When a woman meets an interesting or appealing man, she's thinking about a romantic relationship with him.**

- **When a man meets an attractive and woman, he's wondering what it will take to get in her behind. The challenge begins.**

Men don't fall in love the same way women do and they don't approach sex the same way that women do.

The man DOES NOT fall in love with you once he is allowed to have your body. If he asks like he is in love, it is because he is in love with the new fresh behind in which he was able to partake.

One of the quickest ways to make a man disinterested is to have sex with him early in the relationship.

- **The woman falls in love and becomes emotionally invested when she allows a man to have her body.**

- **A man does not fall in love and become emotionally invested when he is allowed to have a woman's body - especially on the first date or early on right after meeting. The challenge has ended.**

The worst mistake that a woman can make is to fool herself in believing that if she swerves it just right, he'll be hers forever.

A man will only be yours until he's had enough of your swerve and wants some new swerve - especially if he hasn't invested anything to get your swerve like his money, his time, his conversation, etc.

When a Man and A Woman Fall In Love

- A woman does not fall in love and become emotionally invested when she does not let a man have her body.

- A man falls in love and becomes emotionally invested when he earns the right to have a woman's body.

Again... the man falls in love when he DOES NOT get your goodies. The challenge still yet lives.

When it is Easy for a Man or a Woman to Walk Away

- It's easier for a woman to walk away from an unfulfilling relationship with a man if she has never slept with him.

- It's easier for a man to walk away from a woman if he has already tapped her ass.

The whole component of dating is to conduct an interview
- not to conduct intercourse.

This is so basic that it becomes complex if anybody tries to read into it or pick through it.

The Ties that Bind

- A woman's heart is tied to what is between her legs. If she gives it up, she has exposed her heart.

- A man's heart is not tied to his penis. If he gets some, then he just got some. He goes home and washes his penis off and thinks no more about it until he gets hard or horny again.

When a Man Meets a Woman, When a Woman Meets a Man

- When a female meets an interesting or appealing male, she's thinking about a romantic relationship with him.

- When a male meets an attractive and sharp female, he's wondering what it will take to get in her together ass. His challenge begins.

To Recap

- The female falls in love and becomes emotionally invested when she allows a man to have her body.

- A male <u>does not</u> fall in love and become emotionally invested when he is allowed to have a female's body. His challenge is over.

~

- A female does not fall in love and becomes emotionally invested when she does not let a male have her body.

- A male falls in love and becomes emotionally invested when he earns the right to have the body of the female <u>he calls his woman</u>.

~

- It's easier for a female to walk away from an unfulfilling relationship with a male if she has never slept with him because she hasn't given all of herself to him. She hasn't made that ultimate investment to open herself up.

- It's easier for a male to walk away from a female if he was allowed to come into her to let out his deposit, especially without wearing a condom. He got it, he knows what it's like, there's no more wondering.

~

- A woman's heart is tied to her vagina. If she gives it up, she has exposed her heart. Not only that, she has nothing else more of herself to give.

- A man's heart is not tied to his penis. If he gets in her vagina, then that is that - he just got into her vagina. He goes home and washes his stuff off.

ABOUT THE AUTHOR

Tonya Nicol Davis was born in Cleveland, Ohio. Tonya enjoys spending time with her family, traveling, and creating empowerment avenues for women.

Tonya is an accomplished musician, vocalist, voice-over artist, and actor in stage and film. Tonya is the host, executive producer, and musical director for the Internet radio show, "Lady Intelligence Live!"

For more information, please visit: www.ladyintelligence.com.

www.ingramcontent.com/pod-product-compliance
Lightning Source LLC
Chambersburg PA
CBHW020507030426
42337CB00011B/265